AUSTRALIA REMEMBER WHEN

BOB BYRNE

NEWSOUTH

The hustle and bustle of 1960s Melbourne. Life occurred at a slower pace back in the day

INTRODUCTION

This book is a compilation of some of the most popular posts and photos from the 'Australia Remember When' Facebook page and website. It is not meant to be a historical account of growing up in Australia, but rather a nostalgic look back at some of the moments, events, people, personalities and places that were part of an era from the '50s to the '80s. It is completely random, many photos sent from regular readers, some posts inspired by comments –thank you Facebook followers – and others from memories of my own childhood, and in no particular order.

This passion I have for nostalgia goes back to my days as a 'talk-back' and current affairs radio personality, when I started a segment on my daily program where I would play a 'grab' from a news story or a particular event and invite my listeners to call in with their own memories of the occasion. It led to many wonderful on-air moments with an incredible range of emotions, from pure joy and happiness to sorrow, sadness and feelings of great loss.

Until recent times, nostalgia was mainly considered to be unhealthy. Most experts agreed that dwelling on the past rather than living in the present, of comparing how things once were with how they are now, was best avoided and even considered a trigger for depression. Since the turn of this century however, nostalgia is being viewed in a new light and considerable research is being undertaken in the United States and Europe into its possible use as a tool in the battle against anxiety, clinical depression and even Alzheimer's disease.

So, if nostalgia is good for you, let's celebrate!

THOSE WERE THE DAYS

In post-war Australia from the '50s to the '80s, the Baby Boomer era was a time of peace and full employment; of growing consumer demand with a rapidly expanding population driven by a huge immigration program and a birth explosion. Many of us look back today and remember a time of stability, when family life seemed more permanent and secure, everyone seemed to have a job, and income was regular and society more self-assured and harmonious.

Before the sexual revolution of the '60s, marriage was almost universal and marriages endured, people had larger families, most families went to church, felt part of a wider community, ate a family meal each night around the table and seemed more bound by respect and their own family traditions.

As children we enjoyed so much more freedom than the children of today. We were able to roam and engage in all sorts of activities without any adult supervision. During school holidays I recall, on more than one occasion, leaving home early in the morning on my bike, heading off for a day's adventure, and being told to be home before dark, which usually meant before the street lights were switched on. Girls were considered more at risk but even then, it seems our parents held fewer concerns than most parents of today.

Mind you, there was much more discipline, both at school and at home. Corporal punishment was an accepted form of maintaining discipline and sometimes getting the 'cuts' at school would also lead to getting the strap at home because 'you must have done something really wrong for the teacher to have to give you the cane'.

By the '60s the first Baby Boomers were entering their teen years, buying a car and getting a job. Rock 'n' roll was on the transistor radio, the hippie revolution permeated culture and fashions, the Beatles and the Rolling Stones changed music forever, the Vietnam War created deep divisions within the community, the 'Pill' gave women sexual freedom and the sexual revolution arrived.

The '70s saw the end of the Vietnam War and became known as the Whitlam Years. The dismissal of an elected government by the Queen's representative sparked widespread public outrage and was the most controversial event in Australian political history. Indigenous rights were recognised for the first time in Australia's history, the white Australia policy was abolished, multiculturalism was embraced, women's rights were recognised and the environment was acknowledged as an important issue.

Memories!

There is little doubt that most of us look back on our childhood and teenage years with rose-coloured glasses. We avoid, and even bury, unpleasant memories and think only of the good times, the happy times with parents (now perhaps gone), siblings, friends and lovers. Perhaps that is why we love the past so much, it's filled with the good times, the warm memories, the fun, the joy and the laughter.

I hope you will find some of that in these pages: a photo that will tweak a memory, a post that revives a long forgotten, happy event.

Enjoy!

The Big Banana, Coffs Harbour – built in 1964 it's the second big thing ever built in Australia, a year after the Big Scotsman in Medindie, Adelaide

Photo by News Ltd/Newspix

The Big Pineapple, Gympie – opened in 1971 it's not only heritage listed but also claims to be the biggest pineapple on the planet

Photo by Megan Slade/Newspix

There are 'big things' in every state of Australia. The first big thing, the Big Scotsman, was erected in Medindie, Adelaide in 1963 setting off a big-thing trend around the country. With no sign of the public's fascination dwindling, there are now over 150 big things country-wide, with the latest, the Big Bogan, planned for Nyngan in New South Wales in 2016. Primarily built to draw tourists and put placenames on the map, they've become a bit of cult phenomenon with some even being recognised as folk art. Not only that, they've been compared to Egypt's pyramids by some.

The Big Prawn, Ballina – restored in 2013 it now has a tail and weighs in at 35 tonnes

Photo by Robert McKell/Newspix

The Big Ram, Karoonda – completed in 2003 the ram emphasises the importance of sheep in the Mallee region, emphasised even further by its phenomenal weight of 100 tonnes!

Photo by Dean Marzolla/Newspix

The old Sunbeam Mixmaster, I remember it well.
In fact I can still smell sponge mixture even now!

Courtesy of Philip Walkley

Beach Girl Quest, 1954

Photo by News Ltd/Newspix

Philip Walkley shared a photo and some
memories:

An iconic symbol of growing up in the
1960s was the 'Sunbeam – Mixmaster'.
Nothing would ever replace hand-
beating, but boy did we have fun licking
the bowl and the beaters. I remember
making chocolate sponges with this
back in the late 1970s ... apart from the
odd pav Mum hadn't used it since the
mid-80s. Used it the other day and yes,
that 'smell' is still there! It's unique!
What a blessing when the Mixmaster
came along in the '60s! Up until then we
had to use the old hand-beaters. When
making ice cream there was the first lot
of beating, then the mixture was poured
into the metal ice-cream trays and into
the freezer. After a couple of hours we
had to mix it again. This was a pretty
tough job with the old hand-mixer.
When Sunbeam Mixmaster came along,
consumption of homemade ice cream
increased markedly at our place!! And
Mum's sponge cake improved!

Beach Girl Quests at Australian beaches
attracted large crowds back in the 1950s
and '60s. According to the organisers,
entrants were judged on more than just
beauty – poise, charm, deportment,
manner, diction and open-air sports
activities were also appraised.

As one of the contestants commented recently during an ABC broadcast:

We were celebrating freedom. We had the pill. We were celebrating new music, new fashion, and I think we were probably naïve about parading our bodies. It was like almost a reverse part of the women's movement that we were women proud of our bodies and we can wear these little bikinis, get out there and enjoy life and show our bodies off.

There were major prizes to be won including cars and overseas trips.

Obviously today a Miss Beach Girl Quest would be frowned upon. But it was a less discerning time back then!

Students were well-behaved back then, mainly due to fear

Photo by News Ltd/Newspix

Going to school in the '50s, '60s and even '70s was a lot different than it is today!

In those days, teachers had to be treated with the utmost respect, were always addressed as 'Sir' or 'Miss' or by their full title and they generally ruled their classroom with a fist of iron.

I went to a Catholic school where the nuns simply terrified the kids with the constant promise of eternal damnation and a regular caning, whether you deserved it or not, just to keep discipline.

At high school I reckon I got the 'cuts' at least once a day (as did most of the boys), while the girls got the ruler around the legs, mostly for talking in class. I know that in some schools the headmaster usually gave the cane, but at Catholic schools, every nun could give out the cane and parents would not say a word!

What are your memories of going to school?

Coca-Cola yo-yos

Photo by Norm Oorloff/Newspix

Remember the yo-yo craze? The first one I recall would have been in the very late '50s, or maybe early '60s, and then again in the '70s.

Yo-yos have been around for a very long time but sometime in the 1950s, Coca-Cola came up with the idea of using them to promote their soft drink and it really took off.

We had some experts come to our school from the Philippines to show us how to 'rock the cradle' and 'walk the dog' and Coca-Cola used to hold yo-yo competitions in schools and town halls with some pretty valuable prizes for the winners.

I still have my Coca-Cola Russell yo-yo somewhere.

Do you remember your first day at school or kindy?

Unlike today, there was not a lot of pre-school activity back then, like playgroups, kinder-gym and day care, so it was pretty much one day at home as normal with Mum and younger siblings and the next day in a classroom full of complete strangers with this adult stranger out in front of the classroom, telling you to be quiet, not talk and then trying teach you that 1+1=2.

I think that children in that era were expected to stand on their own two feet a bit more and at an earlier age. There was no such thing as 'helicopter parenting'.

I recall my mother coming with me on that first day and I may have shed a tear or two … How about you?

First day at infant school, 1969

Photo by News Ltd/Newspix

'The best example we have seen of the once-prevalent toilet, the Australian "dunny", stands proudly in Falcon Lane, Crows Nest'

Courtesy of Graham and John Waddell

Roger Ray discovered this photo in a book, *Walk Sydney Streets*:

> As a kid growing up, we had an outside toilet with a chain-pull cistern. We used old phone books and newspaper for toilet paper and I don't know what year we went to proper toilet rolls.

> I found this photo in a book called *Walk Sydney Streets* by Alan Waddell who, when in his 90s, walked all over Sydney and suburbs taking thousands of photos which he published in *Walk Sydney Streets*. Sadly, Alan passed away on 2 September 2008. In memory of Alan, his family is maintaining his website and continuing to add accumulated photos of his discoveries.

Isn't this such a typical Australian suburbia backyard of the 1960s with the old outside dunny? Lots of redbacks under the lavatory seat and those 'longdrops' smelled so badly, no wonder they were right down the bottom of the yard!

Nearly every home had a toilet-roll doll in the 1980s

Emlaktuna.com

#1
F A C T

It wasn't until 1984 that 'Advance Australia Fair' became the official national anthem, replacing 'God Save the Queen'. Recommended by the Hawke Government, the Governor–General Sir Ninian Stephen proclaimed it the national anthem on 19 April of that year. Despite being composed by a Scottish-born composer, Peter Dodds McCormick, in the late 19th century Advance Australia Fair had already been chosen as the national song in a 1977 plebiscite.

Laraine Webber shared a photo: 'Does anyone remember having a toilet-roll doll? We made them in high school sewing class.'

Was it an '80s thing? And I think because they were made by kids in class or made and sold to raise money for charity and other worthy causes, almost everyone seemed to have a couple, one in each toilet.

Blue Hills
REVISITED

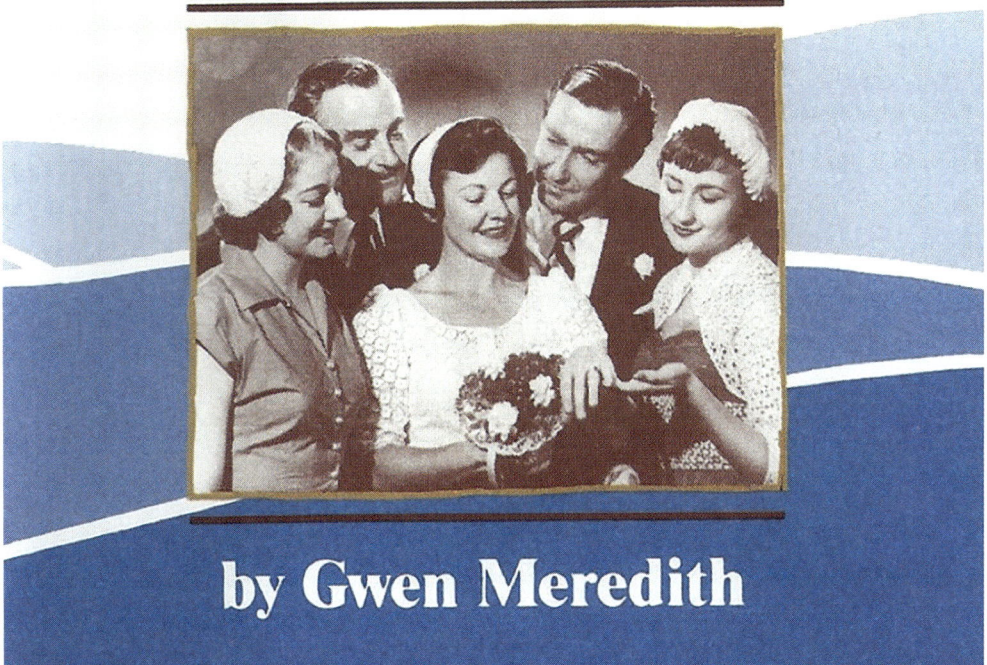

by Gwen Meredith

At 1 o'clock each weekday afternoon the whole of Australia would stop as the first bars of 'Pastorale' were heard on the wireless and it was time for the next episode of 'Blue Hills'.

For almost 30 years it seemed like the whole country would grind to a halt at lunchtime to tune in to their local ABC station and listen to the trials and tribulations of the Gordons and their young family, who lived in a small country town in Tasmania.

Gwen Meredith started writing Blue Hills in 1949 and the final episode went to air in 1976.

> 'I remember as a kid in the 1970s listening to Blue Hills with my Grandmother'
>
> *Courtesy of Michael Brodie*

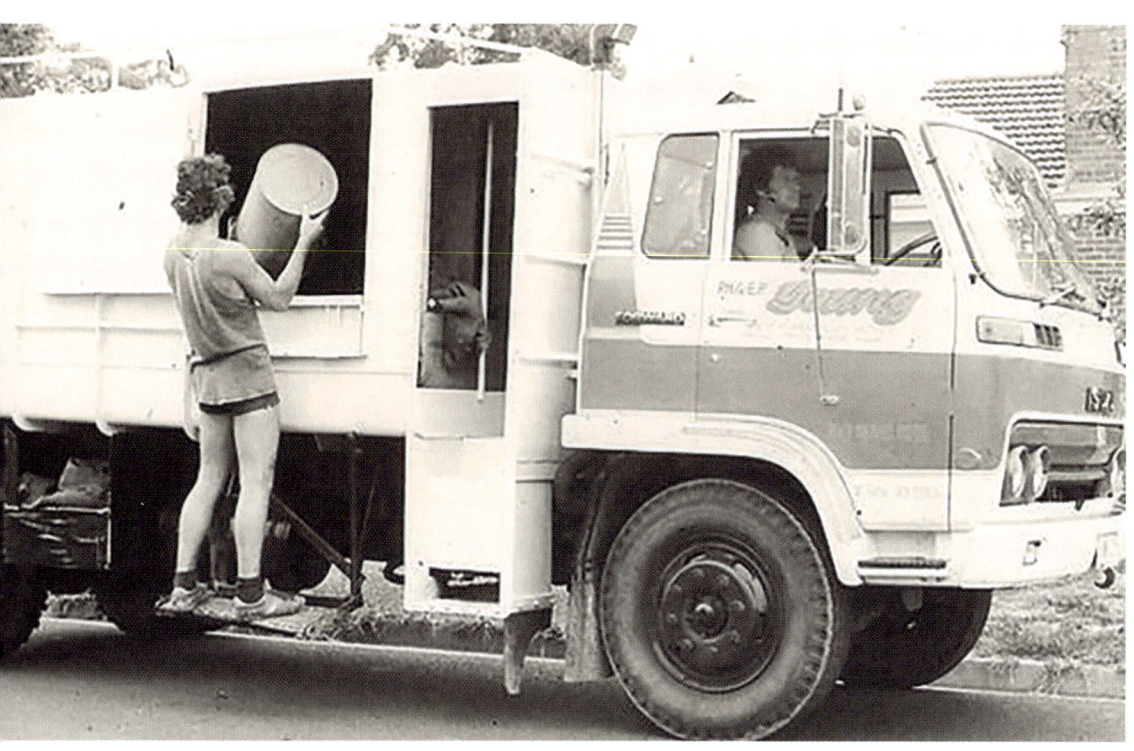

Rubbish was collected by blokes in singlets and
shorts – they'd start banging the metal garbage
bins at about 5am

Casey-Cardinia Library Corporation

Remember when the garbage collection
was done by blokes in singlets and
shorts jumping on and off the truck and
grabbing the old bins?

There'd be three or four garbos
running up and down the street
grabbing the metal bins as they
emptied all the rubbish into the truck.
These days there's the three-bin
system; rubbish, recyclable and green
waste with just one person driving an
air-conditioned truck, operating the
hydraulic arm that lifts the wheelie bins
up to the back of the truck and then
gently puts them back down.

Back in the day they'd be banging
the bins at 5am, waking up the
neighbourhood, the truck revving
up the street and the guys yelling to
one another. At Christmas everyone
would leave beers out for the garbos. It
would've been a tough job, cold and wet
in winter, stinking hot in summer and
I can't recall any of the blokes wearing
protective gear! OH&S would have a fit
if they tried that today.

Natasha Turner shared this photo:

This is my grandfather, Leo van Haasteren. He had a fruit wagon out front of the Adelaide Railway Station on North Terrace for many years. This photo was taken February 1967.

These fruit and vegetable stalls were common in the big traffic areas around the city and suburbs. For many families it was their main source of income and for their customers they offered locally home-grown products in season.

There were also flower stalls, newspaper/magazine kiosks and pie carts dotted around the streets of big cities and towns.

All the produce sold from these barrows would have been freshly picked, weighed and put in brown paper bags for the customers who would have paid in cash.

A totally different experience to buying fruit and veg at the supermarket today.

There was a time when local growers would set up their fruit or flower barrows outside a busy area and sell their home grown produce

Courtesy of Natasha Turner

Legend has it that the first time swimming coach Harry Gallagher saw Dawn Fraser swim in 1953, he wasn't all that impressed. He felt her style was 'rough'.

What did impress him though was that she was able to thrash all the boys at the local swimming pool. Although it took him two years to persuade her to join his squad, within twenty months she was swimming in the 1956 Melbourne Olympics.

And so began the Fraser legend.

Before an ecstatic home crowd, Dawn at just 17, won the 100 metres freestyle in world-record time. She won it again in Rome in 1960 and again in Tokyo in 1964, making her the first of only three swimmers in Olympic history, to have won individual gold medals for the same event.

Dawn won eight Olympic medals in total, including four gold, and six Commonwealth Games gold medals. She also held 39 records.

Dawn always maintained a healthy disregard for authority and had the courage to speak her mind, which endeared her to Australians as a whole.

In 1999 the International Olympics Committee named her the 'World's Greatest Living Female Water Sports Champion'.

World's Greatest Living Female Water Sports Champion

Photo by News Ltd/Newspix

#2
FACT

If you've been on holiday to the Gold Coast in the last 50 years, you probably have a snapshot of yourself with a rainbow lorikeet gripping your head at the Currumbin Wildlife Sanctuary. It all began in 1947, when flower grower and beekeeper Alex Griffiths started feeding the lorikeets to keep them away from his flowers. Before long, a local tourist attraction became a famous bird sanctuary.

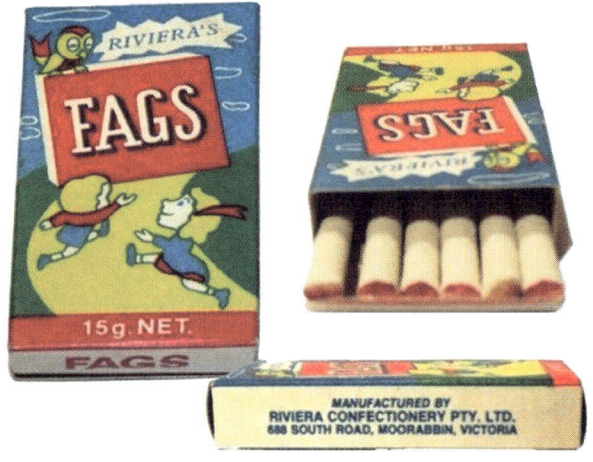

I was a packet-a-day kid! Fags were lolly cigarettes, which we would pretend to smoke when we were growing up

Courtesy of Fyna Foods Australia

Remember 'Fags', the pretend lolly cigarettes?

Very politically incorrect these days, of course. Back in those days, 'fags' was an Aussie slang term for cigarettes. The name was changed to Fads in the early 2000s and they no longer had the little red tip on the end that imitated the lit end of the cigarette either.

I can remember as a kid running around with one hanging out of my mouth pretending to puff on a smoke. As children we all wanted to imitate the grown-ups and we'd all pretend to smoke.

Fortunately, I've never smoked and it's a good thing they changed the name and distanced themselves from promoting cigarettes to children.

Sure brings back memories though!

Remember how much the country was divided as we entered the 1970s?

Support for the Vietnam War was waning as more Australian troops were killed or injured and the moratorium movement began to gather pace.

The protest movement that had started in the '60s gained a new momentum. Left-wing Labor leader Dr Jim Cairns led the moratorium movement in Australia, adopting a strong message of non-violence, and peaceful demonstrations to get the message home to the government of the day. The largest

demonstration took place in Melbourne on 8 May 1970 when more than 100 000 people came together for a peaceful rally, while another 100 000 gathered in the other cities and towns.

What are your memories of the moratorium marches back in 1970?

Thousands gathered on the streets of Melbourne in 1970 and many more gathered in other cities and towns around Australia, to protest over our involvement in the Vietnam War

Photo by News Ltd/Newspix

It might be hard to imagine now but Holden, in the 'golden years' from the '50s to the '80s, was as much a part of Australia as the Sydney Harbour Bridge, beating the Poms at the cricket, football, meat pies and kangaroos. It was part of our DNA.

The first new Holden was launched in 1948 and was an instant hit with the Australian public.

During the '50s, the new Holden dominated the Australian car market with the less expensive four-cylinder cars imported from England and America unable to offer Holden's ability to deal with the rugged rural areas and vast expanses of the country.

Throughout the '60s, '70s and even the '80s, Holden was the car that most Australian families bought or wanted to own. Many people reading this today probably learnt to drive a Holden, bought a second-hand Holden as a teenager, and when they bought a new car, it was probably a Holden. The British had their Jags, the Germans their Mercedez Benz but in Australia, we had the Holden Special!

In those halcyon days, from the '50s right through to the '80s, it would have seemed impossible that one day there would be an Australia without Holden, but as we now know, the seemingly impossible has happened.

After 2017, Holden, Australia's Own Car, will become history.

At least we will have some great memories!

900 000th Holden built in Brisbane, 1962

Photo by Al Pascoe/Newspix

Quintessential Paul Hogan in Sydney, 1983

Photo by News Ltd/Newspix

#3
FACT

A generation of Australians can't spot a pelican without calling out, 'Mr Percival! Mr Percival!' – all thanks to Henri Safran's 1976 film *Storm Boy*, based on Colin Thiele's book. Mr Percival's antics weren't computer-generated – this pelican really could catch a ball! He lived a long life, dying of old age at the Adelaide Zoo in 2009.

I'll never forget the night I saw Paul Hogan on TV for the first time.

It was on a talent program, an early version I guess of 'Australia's Got Talent'. It was in black and white of course and the year would have been '72 or '73. Hoges won the heat of course with his act ... playing a 'garbophone', which was an instrument he'd invented made from a plastic garbage bin.

Shortly thereafter he was given his own comedy program, 'The Paul Hogan Show', which ran from 1973 to 1984, was hugely popular and genuinely funny.

During the early 1980s, Hoges filmed a series of television ads promoting Australia in the United States with the 'Throw another shrimp on the barbie' line and which were very successful. And who could forget Mick 'Crocodile' Dundee in the 1986 film!

Onya Hoges!!

There was a time when Australia had inspectors who patrolled the beach and ordered people to cover up in the name of public decency.

The bikini was launched by the swimwear designer Paula Stafford back in 1952, causing an uproar at the time.

Legally, swimming costumes had to be at least three inches long in the leg and cover the front of the body all the way to the armpits.

At Bondi beach, one month after the introduction of the bikini, the infamous beach inspector, Aub Laidlaw, escorted a 17-year-old back to the Pavillion because her clothing did not meet the regulation.

The last recorded skirmish on the beach was in 1961 when Miss Joan Barry was ordered from the beach and fined £3 for 'offensive behaviour'.

Thank goodness we got over that!

Beach inspector Aub Laidlaw inspects a bikini to make sure it meets 'public decency' standards at Bondi, 16 November 1958

Fairfax Syndication

When Bob Menzies retired from politics in 1966, he was not only our longest-serving Prime Minister but for half the population, he was the only Prime Minister we had ever known.

He was the father figure for generations of Australians, the man who led us through the '50s and '60s and steered the country through the best and the worst of times.

There have been many words written about this colossus of politics, a man who loved the Queen and cricket. As one Canberra columnist once wrote: 'Menzies knew in the fifties and sixties that what he was required to do to govern Australia was to do nothing. That was the Menzies masterpiece.'

Before he left office, Bob Menzies committed Australia to the war in Vietnam and conscription – possibly for the Boomer generation, the two worst decisions he'd ever made while in office.

Menzies was PM for a total of 18 years

Photo by News Ltd/Newspix

25

'Farewell me little lovelies!' Farewell Aunty Jack was inspired by Grahame Bond's real life Uncle Jack who he really disliked as a child

Photo by News Ltd/Newspix

Although it only ran for a couple of seasons the Aunty Jack Show on ABC TV attained a cult status that persists today.

Aunty Jack was devised by actor and comedian Grahame Bond and was inspired by his real-life overbearing Uncle Jack, his grandfather and a little bit by the tea ladies at the ABC.

Aunty Jack was quite a unique character, a transvestite with a gravel voice and a big moustache who wore a big tent dress, a single boxing glove, footy socks and work boots. She rode a Harley-Davidson motorbike and was always threatening to 'rip yer bloody arms off'.

The show was very controversial right from episode one and after two seasons Grahame decided to kill off the show by having Aunty Jack die of a heart attack, although she did make a brief comeback in 1975 for an ABC special.

THEIR DAY ON THE MOON

EARLY today Neil Armstrong and Edwin Aldrin were dozing in the Eagle after their historic two-hour walk on the moon.

They were due to blast off at 3.55 a.m. to rejoin the Columbia command ship after 21 hours 7 minutes on the Sea of Tranquillity.

Picture below shows the two astronauts in front of the Eagle on the moon. ● The moon story, other pictures inside.

BUREAU SAYS: Further showers. Local hail. Some snowfalls. Squally south-west winds. ● Weather details are on Page 37.

The Sun
NEWS - PICTORIAL
Registered in Australia for transmission by post as a newspaper
44 FLINDERS ST. PHONE 63-0211 By Air 6c **5c**

14,603. Melbourne, Tuesday, July 22, 1969. 52 Pages

'That's one small step for man, one giant leap for mankind'

Photo by News Ltd/Newspix

Where were you on Monday, 21 July 1969? In what is one of the most famous moments in human history Neil Armstrong stepped off *Eagle*, the lunar landing module, on to the surface of the moon, becoming the first human to walk on its surface. And 600 million people worldwide could watch it all on their TVs with the help of Parkes radio telescope in western New South Wales. Despite terrible weather and some technical difficulties those grainy black and white images are still etched in the memories of those who watched it.

The Kodak 'Box Brownie' must have been one of the first cameras on the market back in the 1950s. My father bought one so he could record such occasions as the first day at school, first communion and various family events. Mind you, in those days you did not take too many photos as you could not afford the cost of getting films developed!

From memory, there were eight photos per roll of black and white film, with a self-winder and you had to make *very* sure that you didn't wind past the number in the little round red window because you could *not* rewind it back 'just a bit'. Film was somewhat costly and it took about two weeks to get the eagerly awaited photos back from the chemist, with the inevitable 'bad' or blurred shot that you reluctantly tossed away.

Amazing how far photography has progressed in 60 years!

This is the sort of camera I can remember my father having in the '50s

Wikipedia, photo NotFromUtrecht

Remember when doing the weekly grocery shop was a far more personal experience?

Back before the major supermarkets came along, most of the everyday staples were purchased at the local grocer's shop, where the man and his wife who owned the shop (and their children too), stood behind the counter, sometimes in white dust coats, and served their customers personally.

They would know each customer's name, usually be aware of what they required, would package everything in

Remember when telephones were used just to make telephone calls?

These old bakelite phones were about in the '50s and '60s when many private homes didn't even have the phone on. I personally recall that if there was a reason to make a phone call, and it needed to be a *good* reason, we used to have to go to the nearest public phone or to a neighbour who might just have had one of these old black phones. Manual telephone exchanges were phased out in the mid-1950s as we moved to telephones with self dial, but if you had to make a trunk call or even an overseas call, that still required you to go through the trunk exchange.

How different to the mobile phones we now have, which are in effect a computer you can hold in the palm of your hand.

Kids helping their Dad in his grocery shop, 1950

Photo by News Ltd/Newspix

The original old bakelite telephone – similar to the one we first got at home, probably in the early '60s

dreamstime

brown paper bags or wrap them from a large ream of brown paper with a big cutter on the front. The paper would be saved for later school projects and the like.

Sometimes they would sell groceries 'on tick' if they knew their customer was doing it tough, or they would home deliver to make life a bit easier.

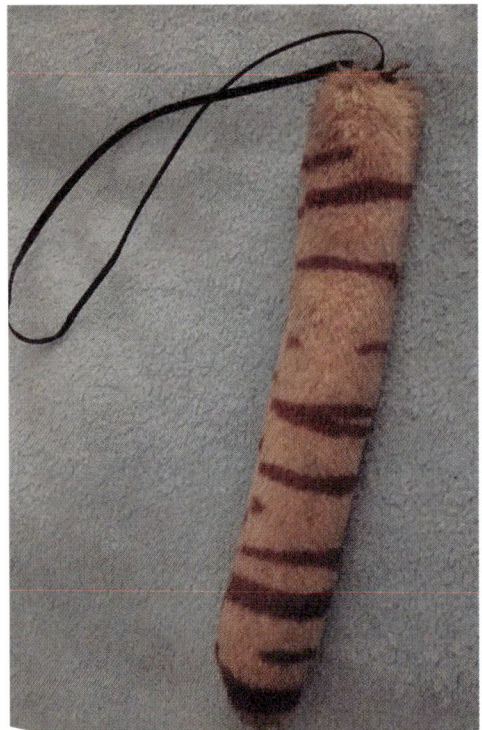

'Put a Tiger in Your Tank' and hang the tiger tail from the car aerial

Courtesy of Kevin Brown

It's truly amazing what people hang on to and the photos of memorabilia that people send in. For example, Kevin Brown sent in this photo: 'Who remembers the tiger's tails from Esso service stations?'

That's Kevin's tail, which he still has after all these years. Esso had the slogan 'Put a Tiger in Your Tank' and I can't quite recall now whether they gave these away or whether you had to buy them. I remember kids getting them for their bikes also.

Amoco had 'the final filter' and it's always been 'Go Well, Go Shell'.

#4
FACT

On 27 May 1967 a referendum was held to determine whether two references in the Constitution that discriminated against Aboriginal people should be removed. The first clause allowed the Federal Parliament to make laws for the 'people of any race, other than the aboriginal people in any State, for whom it is necessary to make special laws.' The second stated that Aboriginal people could not be counted in any census. It resulted in the highest YES vote ever recorded in a Federal referendum, with 90.77 per cent voting for change.

Michael and Lindy Chamberlain talking to the
media in 1980 soon after a dingo had taken their
baby Azaria

Photo by News Ltd/Newspix

It was the case that divided Australia!

Was Lindy Chamberlain guilty of murdering her baby daughter, Azaria, or did a dingo snatch her as the family claimed?

The Chamberlain family was on a camping trip to Uluru (it was known as Ayers Rock back then) and stayed in the public camping ground. On the night of 17 August 1980 Lindy said she had seen a dingo coming out of the tent, and when she checked on Azaria the infant was gone.

Lindy and Michael Chamberlain reported that she had been taken from their tent by a dingo.

Her body was never found.

The first Coroner's Inquest confirmed that a dingo had killed Azaria but that verdict was later overturned, and Lindy was tried for murder and spent more than three years in prison. She was released when a piece of Azaria's clothing was found and a new inquest was opened.

Thirty-two years after Azaria's death in 2012 the Chamberlains' version of events was officially confirmed by a coroner.

To this day you will find people who think the dingo was innocent!

Children playing in the school playground in
1954–55. There would be games like 'chasey',
'hidey', cricket, ball games and a bit of friendly
wrestling

Museum Victoria. Reg. No: MM 104103

Kim Bell shared a memory about playing
chasey at school:

When we were kids we'd all run around
chasing each other right through morning
and afternoon recess and during lunch
hour too.

The rules were very simple, one kid
was chosen to go 'he' or 'it' and they had

The old Speedie toaster, just like the one we had at home

Courtesy of Sarah Louise Bowshall

I was toasting some bread this morning and as I stood waiting for the toast to pop up, I was thinking back to how we used to make toast back in Boomer times.

I recall even before we had a toaster, my father had a long-handled prongs that he would stick the bread on and hold it over the hot coals in the wood stove until it toasted. Occasionally he would drop one in the fire.

Then we got an electric toaster that had sprung metal sides that opened. You'd put the bread in, and when you thought one side would be done, you'd open the flap thingy and turn the bread over to toast the other side.

The element would burn out every so often, but they could be replaced simply, just like the element in the electric jug.

I think if my modern toaster or electric kettle stopped working, it would be a whole lot cheaper to chuck them out and buy new ones rather than having them repaired!

We live in a throw-away world nowadays.

to chase all the other kids all over the playground until they tagged or touched one saying 'you're he' and then that kid would be 'it'.

Or we might play hidey or hide 'n 'seek (I'm sure you remember the rules). What are some of your schoolyard memories?

'Dame Edna Everage', Sydney, 1983

Photo by John Burney/Newspix

Kim Bell shared a memory about Dame Edna:

It's hard to believe that Barry Humphries first introduced Dame Edna back in the mid-1950s. In the '80s all of my friends used to do the Dame Edna thing, we'd talk about sling back shoes, diamante glasses and wisteria blue rinses.

Dame Edna was originally a rather drab Moonee Ponds housewife, satirising Australian suburbia, but as time went on, she adopted a far more outlandish wardrobe with her lilac-coloured hair and 'cat-eye' glasses.

Following several film appearances and an elevation to Damehood in the 1970s, she became 'Housewife and Superstar', then a 'Megastar' and finally 'Gigastar'.

Throughout the 1980s and 1990s Dame Edna became increasingly known and popular in North America after a number of stage and television appearances.

I believe she has been semi-retired by Barry Humphries, but still pops up occasionally on the telly.

We grew up with her and loved her, how about you?

#5
FACT

Meeting the love of your life can be difficult ... remember when we had country B&S balls to help us on our way before internet dating came along? Dancing, drinking, fancy frocks and a sit-down dinner, and a bumpy ride home in the ute before the time of liquor laws. Although many would just set up their swag and sleep it off in the ute.

Prince Leonard of the Principality of Hutt River
in his official royal regalia, 1975

Photo by News Ltd/Newspix

Who said Australia doesn't have its own royals? Prince Leonard (aka Leonard George Casley) has ruled over the Western Australian Principality of Hutt River since the early '70s when Casley seceded from the State of Western Australia over a dispute with the State Government on wheat production quotas. Casley declared independence from the Commonwealth of Australia on 21 April 1970. It all seemed to be a bit tongue-in-cheek at first but Prince Leonard turned out to be more than a match for the barrage of Federal and State Government lawyers who tried to close the newly declared province down. Hutt River started to mint and print its own money, award honours and was recognised by a small number of countries as a 'micro-nation'. Not surprisingly, the Australian Government does not recognise the secession of Hutt River!

Neville Bonner, 1971

Photo by News Ltd/Newspix

In 1971 Neville Bonner AO became the first Indigenous Australian to sit as a member of the Parliament of Australia.

Mr Bonner was an elder for the Jagera people and was initially appointed by the Queensland Parliament to fill a casual vacancy in the representation of Queensland in the Senate. He later became the first Indigenous Australian to be elected by popular vote and sat in Parliament from 1972 to 1983.

In 1979 Neville Bonner became Australian of the Year, along with naturalist Harry Butler, and a year later was appointed an Officer of the Order of Australia.

He died at Ipswich in 1999, aged 76.

I was 'on air' doing my morning radio talk show at 2GO Gosford on the morning of 18 January 1977 when news came through that a crowded commuter train in Sydney had slammed into the supports of an overhead bridge at Granville, a suburb in Western Sydney. People were trapped and dying inside the crushed train. The huge weight of the bridge had collapsed onto two of the train's passenger carriages and frantic efforts were being made to rescue those trapped inside. We crossed live to the scene and for the rest of the day tried our best to keep audiences informed about the rescue efforts, which continued on for many hours.

There were heartbreaking stories of loss and heroism right throughout the day and in the end 83 people lost their lives, more than 210 were injured, and 1300 people were affected.

Australia's worst rail disaster occurred back in 1977 at Granville in New South Wales

Photo by News Ltd/Newspix

Donald Campbell was a character straight out of the pages of a 'Boys Own Annual'.

He arrived in Australia in 1964 to take on both the world land speed record and water speed records and on 17 July he set the speed record on the dry salt pan of Lake Eyre in his famous Bluebird car.

Later that year he would smash all expectations and take both the world land and water speed records, a feat that has yet to be matched in a single year.

He broke the water speed world record on Lake Dumbleyung near Perth, Western Australia, on the last day of 1964.

Tragedy struck just three years later, when his craft flipped as he attempted another water-speed record in January 1967 on Coniston Water in England.

His body was finally found by divers in 2010, and his remains were buried with his family.

Donald Campbell's Bluebird racing car

Photo by News Ltd/Newspix

The old Pizza Hut. On a Saturday night you could eat as much pizza as you liked and keep topping up your ice-cream bowl

Courtesy of Pizza Hut Australia

Remember those early dine-in buffet style Pizza Huts?

When Pizza Hut first opened in Australia in the '70s, you could actually go for a sit-down meal, grab as much pizza as you wanted to eat with plenty of drinks to go around and fill your ice-cream bowl to the brim and coat it with all sorts of toppings.

I'm not sure when they became takeaway only fast food place, but I know that the traditional 'hut' style buildings have all but disappeared these days.

Who can recall going out as a family to Pizza Hut for the night and serving yourself from the buffet?

The first credit card to be introduced into Australia was Bankcard in 1974

Wikipedia

Can you remember what life was like before credit cards?

Everyone was paid in cash and on payday, you lined up with your co-workers to get your pay envelope. Then it was off to the bank or off to the various places where you owed money, to pay your bills, in cash, usually by lining up at the counter. I think it may have been in the '70s that most companies started depositing pays directly into bank accounts.

And then Bankcard came along. It was a shared-brand credit card issued by the banks in Australia between 1974 and 2006.

Before that time, only store cards, Diners Club and American Express were available and these were either restrictive or only accessible to the wealthy. Bankcard was eventually superseded by Visa and MasterCard and nowadays hardly anybody has cash in their wallet, mainly just plastic cards.

And you simply wave your credit card at the terminal now and everything is approved, no waiting!

Australi

"Gee Billy, I wish I

They don't make Polly Waffles any-more. Damn!

Do you remember the original Polly Waffle when it was made by Hoadleys?

Brief history: the first Polly Waffle was made in Melbourne in 1947. During the 1970s the advertising slogan for Polly Waffle was 'mmm, crunch, aah!' It was a big seller for Hoadleys back then. In 1972, Hoadley's Chocolates was acquired by Rowntree's and in 1988, Nestlé acquired Rowntree's.

In mid-2009 a new recipe for Polly Waffle was released along with new packaging, but while the new product had the same appearance it was more sugary and had a more brittle wafer.

Nestlé announced on 23 November 2009 that Polly Waffle was being discontinued after 62 years, due to poor sales.

Gee, I'd love an original Polly Waffle right now!

The original wrappers for Polly Waffle and Violet Crumble at 8d each

Pinterest

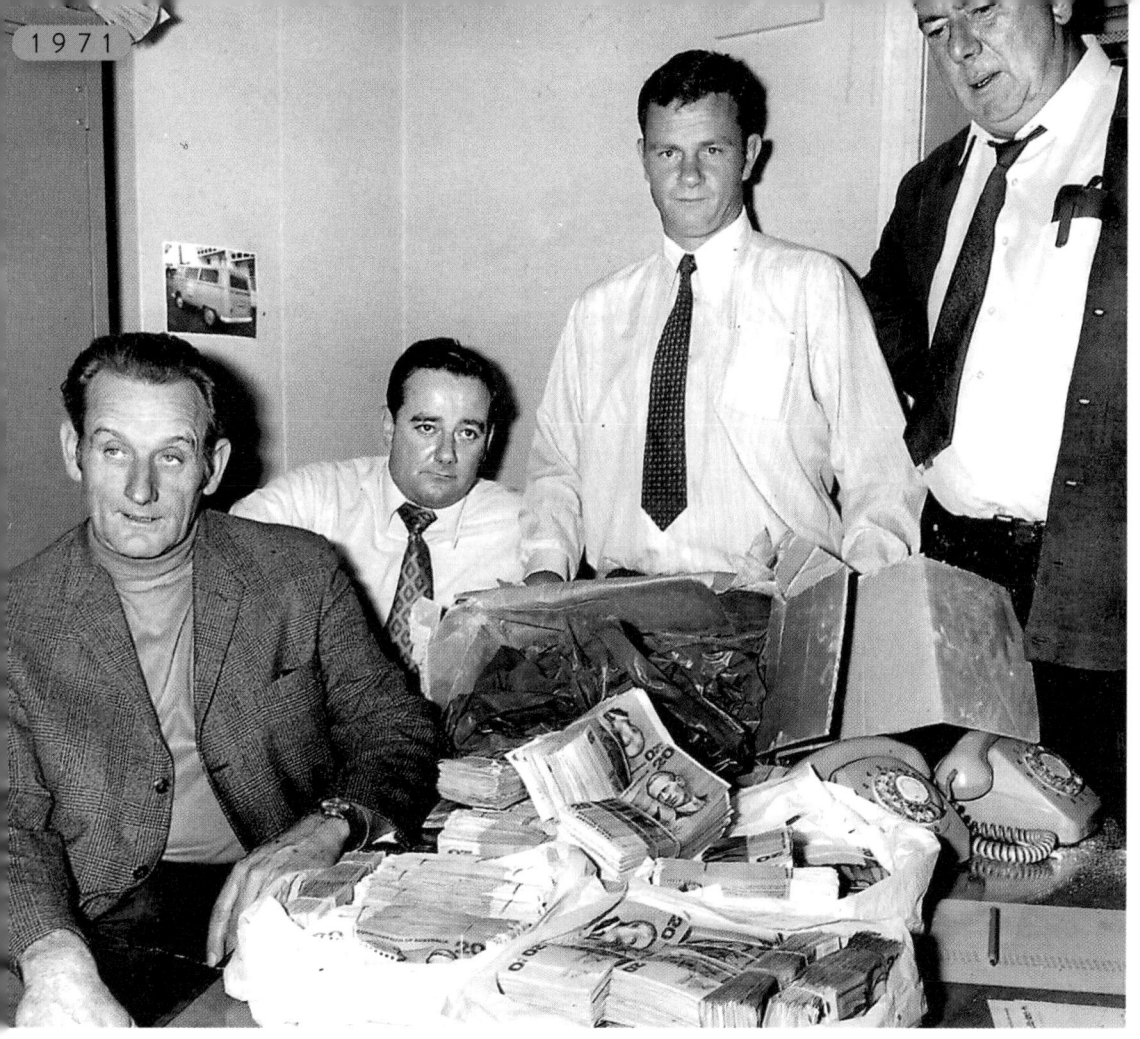

Unamused detectives with the extortionate
amount of $500 000 demanded by Mr Macari,
aka 'Mr Brown'

Photo by News Ltd/Newspix

It was called 'The Great Plane Robbery of 1971'. On 26 May that year, a 'Mr Brown' called the federal police claiming Qantas flight 755 from Sydney to Hong Kong, with 128 passengers on board, was carrying a bomb. Mr Brown warned that the bomb would detonate if the plane descended below 6500 metres, and that he would reveal the bomb's location for the modest sum of $500 000. The plane returned to Sydney and circled for several hours while authorities scrambled to hand the money over. With cash in hand Mr Brown phoned police informing them that it was all a hoax and that the plane could safely land. The real culprit, Peter Macari, was arrested and charged on multiple counts later that year.

Catching tadpoles was big in the 1950s!

Photo by News Ltd/Newspix

Watching my grandchildren playing with their iPads and digital devices, I'm left pondering how much childhood has changed so much in just three generations.

I'm convinced that growing up in those Boomer years, from the middle of last century, allowed us to have a far happier, less-complicated upbringing with considerably more freedom than any child of today.

Saturday afternoons and school holidays meant freedom. We'd be out on our bikes from early morning, riding to the creek for a 'skinny dip' or catching some tadpoles that we'd bring home in a jar, hoping to watch them grow into frogs.

Another favourite destination was an old, long-abandoned fort built during the war where we'd engage in war games, climb steep cliffs and dig tunnels in the old quarry.

An extra regular stamping ground was the beach where we'd swim, dive off the jetty and for lunch have a Bush biscuit with Vegemite from the little kiosk. What are some of your best memories from childhood?

#6
FACT

Remember Captain Fortune? The 'Captain Fortune Show' was the first kids' TV show to air in Australia beginning in 1957. Without any rehearsal the show was done in front of a live audience. Alan Herbert's character Captain Fortune wore a false beard and naval uniform, and spoke directly with the kids. Because the show was broadcast live, and never taped, sadly no film copies of the Captain Fortune Show exist.

The Old Tin Shed in Elizabeth Street stood next to the GPO

Photo by News Ltd/Newspix

Remember The Old Tin Shed in the centre of Melbourne?

Right up until the middle '60s, a suburban-style motor accessories store stood at one of the Melbourne CBD's prime locations.

It was known for years as 'The Old Tin Shed' and was situated on the corner of Elizabeth and Little Bourke streets, right next to the iconic GPO.

Originally built in 1906, the shed was intended to be on the site temporarily, but it became something of a city landmark despite persistent calls for it to be removed.

Allan W. Taylor & Co. operated a successful business for motor accessories and tools from the shed and eventually vacated the premises in the early 1960s.

The Old Tin Shed was finally removed in 1964.

Don Bradman, 'The Don', is widely acknowledged as the greatest Test batsman of all time. Bradman's career 'test batting' average of 99.94 is often cited as the greatest achievement ever by any sportsman in any major sport. In fact, statistics show that he was just about twice as good as any of his peers.

The story that the young Bradman practised alone with a cricket stump and a golf ball hit up against a galvanised iron tank is part of Australian folklore. If he had hit just one more six in a test match, he would have had the incredible average of a century for every innings.

By the time I got to play cricket at school, The Don had retired but his legend will live on for as long as the game is played!

The Don, 1934

Photo by News Ltd/Newspix

A kitbag or Gladstone bag, everyone's Dad or grandfather had one

Wikipedia, photo davidd

There was a time when getting your first kitbag or Gladstone bag was almost like a time-honoured passage into young adulthood for boys.

From memory, most boys got their first kitbag when they started high school. Up until then we had a school bag, but going into first year of high school we had a new kitbag, all polished and firm. After a few years the leather would soften and the kitbag would then be quite soft and floppy.

My father took his lunch to work every day in his floppy old kitbag, which he must have had for years. Although they got floppy you never needed a new one because they always did the job.

Sadly these days nobody uses kitbags anymore, now everyone has a backpack. Just another great old tradition that's probably been lost forever.

Remember when the laminex and chrome tables and chairs first hit the market ... maybe late in the 1950s?

I remember my mother ditching the beautiful old solid wooden dining suite (probably mahogany or oak) and replacing it with a yellow laminex setting, complete with chrome chairs with yellow and black padded seats.

From memory, nobody wanted to buy the old solid wooden table and it was probably cut up for firewood in the end because everybody else was also getting rid of their traditional tables and chairs in favour of the new laminex products. I shudder to think about how much traditional old furniture was destroyed and replaced with plastic and chrome at that time!

To be fair, there are lots of people who love the retro look of laminex furniture.

Do you remember the laminex craze?

It was back in the '50s when laminex and chrome became all the rage

Courtesy of Jess Mallia

The Rubiks cube drove many a kid to distraction back in the '80s!

Wikipedia, photo Booyabazooka

#7
FACT

The Rubiks cube first appeared in the early '80s and immediately became the biggest craze in Australia. Originally called the Magic Cube, it was invented by a professor of architecture Ernő Rubik. It was not only popular with kids but adults as well.

Legend has it that the professor had no idea that he had created a puzzle until the first time he scrambled his new cube and then tried to put it back together. He had really invented it as a teaching tool to help his students understand 3D objects.

I notice these days you can watch videos on YouTube to help you solve the puzzle of getting all the colours back together, but when it first came out there were no instructional videos, you just had to try and figure it out yourself.

I was given one but must admit I never had the patience to sit down and try and figure it out.

How about you?

Many of us can't start the day without an espresso, latte, flat white or cappuccino. When did this obsession begin? In the 1930s and '40s, Greek and Italian migrants brought café culture to Australia. Greek immigrant Sam Akon Economopoulos introduced espresso machines to his Sydney milk bars – Patricia's – in 1948. In 1954, the famous Pelligrini's espresso bar opened in Melbourne, and so the coffee obsession was born.

Graham Kennedy was the greatest TV entertainer Australia has ever produced!

Photo by News Ltd/Newspix

He was the genuine king of television. I remember some of his outrageously hilarious TV skits with either Bert Newton or one of the other cast members of the 'In Melbourne Tonight' team.

Graham started out in radio and after a guest appearance on a Red Cross TV fundraiser, he was selected to front a variety show that Channel 9 in Melbourne had planned. It was never really envisaged that the show would last more than maybe a few months but Graham was pure magic in front of the camera and before long he got a weekly show, which was then increased to two shows. By 1965 IMT reached its 2000th instalment and more people watched the show per capita than any other television program in the world! I love to watch some of Kennedy's skits even now and you can also catch some of his skits on YouTube.

He was the king.

Who played marbles as a kid?

More popular with boys, marbles (also called alleys), was a pretty serious game.

Cats eyes from memory were the most common, trombolas were the big ones, the white marbles with the red splash were called blood trackers and ball bearings were also used and were known

as 'steelies'. There were also 'bottlers', clear glass marbles that were originally used to seal the old cool drink bottles.

There were several different games of marbles. You could also play 'keeps', which meant the winner kept the loser's marble (disaster if it was one of your favourites), or not keeps, just a friendly game.

He was always in the Sunday comics – Ginger Meggs was a typical Aussie kid when we were growing up

Photo by News Ltd/Newspix

As kids we would eagerly look forward to the comics in the paper every Sunday and Ginger Meggs was a 'must' read. He was the Bart Simpson of our era! Everybody at some stage knows a Ginger Meggs, a pesky, red-haired freckle-faced kid and a real little mischief-maker.

Ginger Meggs is still Australia's most popular, and now longest-running, comic strip. This little Aussie larrikin was first created in the 1920s by Jimmy Bancks.

Two feature films, four stage plays and more than fifty 'annuals' have been made about Ginger Meggs. It also made his creator, J.C. Bancks, the highest paid black and white artist or journalist around at the time.

Ginger Meggs is the longest-running and most popular comic strip in Australian history and is now read in 34 countries around the world!

Two boys playing a pretty serious game of marbles

Museum Victoria Reg. No: MM 104111

When I think back to the '70s, the dominant images that come to mind are the 'Its Time' advertising campaign, which helped Gough Whitlam win government in 1972, and the other image is of the Governor–General's emissary, David Smith, reading the proclamation on the steps of Parliament House, dismissing the Whitlam Government in 1975.

By the early '70s, many Australians had grown tired of the Liberal government of the day. They had been in power for over 20 years and the mood, especially amongst Baby Boomers, was one for change.

Gough Whitlam, leader of the Labor Party was an imposing figure on the Australian political scene. Helped enormously by the very successful 'Its Time' TV campaign and supported by some of the country's foremost performers, he was swept into office. Alison McCallum was the lead singer for the 'Its Time' jingle with the chorus comprising a 'Who's Who' of Australian entertainment, including Barry Crocker, Bert Newton, Bobby Limb, Dawn Lake, Col Joye, Grahame Kennedy, Jack Thompson, Jackie Weaver, Jimmy Hannan, Judy Stone and Little Pattie.

Just three years later came the dismissal of the Whitlam Government by the Governor–General, Sir John Kerr, in the climax of the constitutional crises.

No matter what your politics, I think you will have to agree that Gough Whitlam epitomised the Baby Boomer generation back in the '70s – young, aggressive and hungry for change!

David Smith announces the dismissal of the Whitlam Government while Gough looks on

Photo by Guy Wilmott/Newspix

Gough Whitlam and singer Little Pattie sporting 'It's Time' t-shirts

Photo by Graeme Fletcher/Newspix

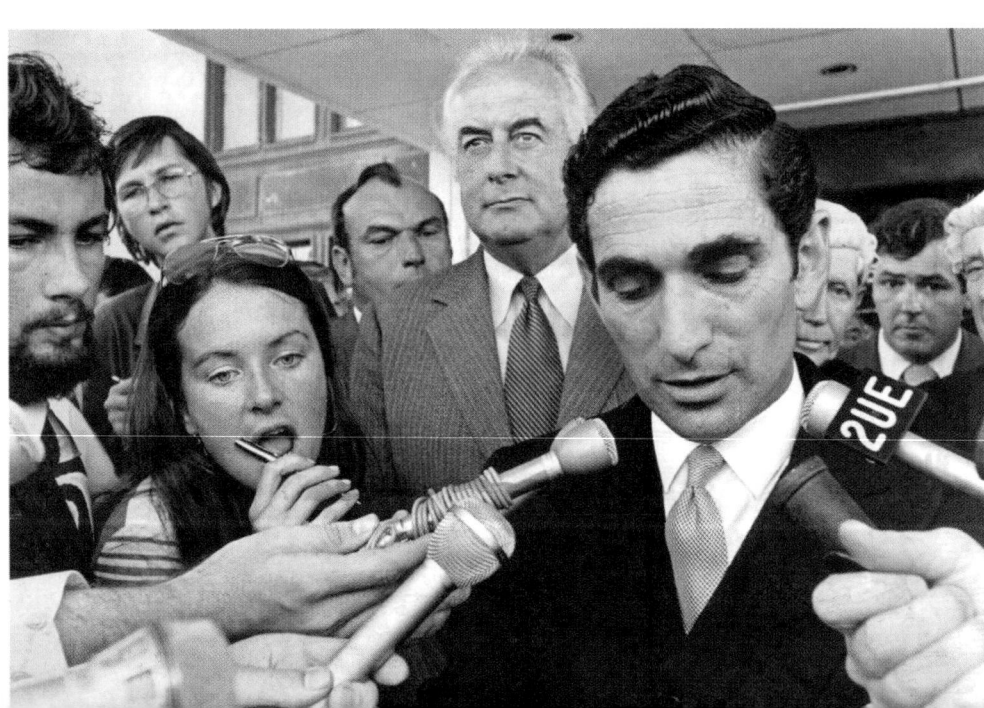

1972

Shopping for Father's Day at Coles, 1950

Photo by News Ltd/Newspix

Do you remember Coles before it became a giant supermarket chain?

Back in the '60s, Coles was more like some of the $2 stores about today but with merchandise exhibited from waist-high display counters. The shop assistants

would patrol up and down between the counters to serve you when you wanted to make a purchase.

This photo should bring back a few memories of shopping with Mum! Coles had its own 'Embassy' and 'Starlet' brands.

After shopping it would be up to the first floor to Coles Cafeteria for lunch, or maybe down the street to one of the other tea rooms.

'Pick-a-Box' host Bob Dyer (*centre*) Barry Jones (*right*)

Photo by News Ltd/Newspix

Remember when a young Barry Jones became known as the 'National Quiz King of Australia'?

Barry was a Melbourne school teacher and became a household name in the 1960s when he won the title of national quiz champion on Bob Dyer's BP 'Pick-a-Box' show on Channel 7 in the days of black-and-white television.

Barry was a great TV performer and to win the title, he beat challengers from the US, UK, Finland, South Africa, and elsewhere. He eventually turned to federal politics in 1997 and was Minister for Science from 1983 to 1990 and national president of the Australian Labor Party from 1992 to 2000.

The most memorable moment was when Barry actually challenged Bob Dyer over the answer to a question about the Governor-General of India. Turned out Barry was right (as usual).

#8
FACT

The 1943 controversy surrounding the Archibald prize-winning portrait of fellow artist Joshua Smith by painter William Dobell, ended up in court. Opponents of the win alleged that it was not a portrait, but a caricature. Dobell's supporters disagreed and the artist himself said he was trying to 'create something instead of copying something'. Justice Roper upheld Dobell's award.

Benny, Anni-Frid, Agnetha and Björn became one of the most successful popular-music groups in the world, topping the charts worldwide from 1975 to 1982

Wikipedia

Whenever we remember the '70s, the one pop group that comes to mind is ABBA.

They toured Australia in 1977, had a massive number of hit songs and took the country by storm!

The whole tour and its subsequent *ABBA: The Movie* produced some ABBA lore, as well. Agnetha Fältskog's blonde good looks had long made her the band's 'pin-up girl', a role she apparently hated.

During the Australian tour, she performed in a skin-tight white jumpsuit, causing one Australian newspaper to use the headline 'Agnetha's bottom tops dull show'. When asked about this at a news conference, she replied: 'Don't they have bottoms in Australia?'

REFRIGERATORS · ELECTRIC STOVES **WALTONS** RADIOGRAMS WAS

TEMPORARY WALTONS CENTRE

Waltons Store, Parramatta, 1954

Mitchell Library, State Library of New South Wales, d7-43278

There have been many names in retail that have disappeared over the past 50 years, names such as Waltons and Fosseys.

Waltons had 12 stores around Melbourne and Victoria, and over 60 stores across the eastern states, including Sydney, Brisbane and numerous suburban and country outlets. They also operated several stores in South Australia.

Waltons started out as a menswear shop in George Street in Sydney but expanded rapidly by buying up smaller retailers and by 1972 they had 96 department stores.

Norm, the star of the 'Life. Be in it' campaigns of the 1970s and 1980s

Courtesy of Life. Be in it

Remember when the old 'Life. Be in it' ad campaign first started?

The idea was to create a message that asked the couch-potato TV viewer to 'get up, turn off the telly and go for a walk'.

The main character, Norm, was a middle-aged man with a prominent beer gut – meant to represent a 'normal' Australian and to help us see there is probably a bit of Norm in all of us. Like a lot of Aussies he makes his point in a light-hearted way that got it across.

It was created in the mid-70s and became one of the most enduring and widely recognised lifestyle messages in Australia.

I haven't seen Norm on TV for a while now, but maybe it's time to bring him back, what do you think?

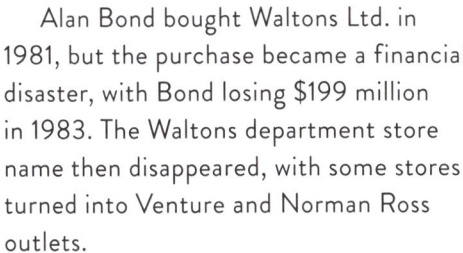

Alan Bond bought Waltons Ltd. in 1981, but the purchase became a financial disaster, with Bond losing $199 million in 1983. The Waltons department store name then disappeared, with some stores turned into Venture and Norman Ross outlets.

Affectionately known as 'Ding Dong', Denise Drysdale is a much-loved TV presenter

Photo by Barry Sprosen/Newspix

She is one of Australia's favourite TV personalities, affectionately known to everyone as 'Ding Dong'.

Denise Drysdale started her career when she was just a child as a dancer on stage and at just 17 became Melbourne's first go-go dancer when she landed a gig on the TV show 'Kommotion'.

In 1974, she became Ernie Sigley's barrel girl on 'The Ernie Sigley Show' and it was here she gained the nickname Ding Dong.

In 1975, Denise won the TV Week Gold Logie award for the 'Most Popular Female Personality on Australia TV'. She won her second Gold Logie the following year and in the same period, won consecutive Silver Logies.

Over the years, she has appeared regularly on numerous television shows and remains one of our favourite TV personalities.

There was tremendous excitement around the nation when the Melbourne Olympics commenced 22 November 1956.

Although there was concern that the Games would not go ahead because of bickering between Federal and State politicians, the final result was a triumph for Australia.

The major events were centred around the Melbourne Cricket Ground and in terms of gold medals, were one of the most successful ever for Australian athletes.

Competitors such as Betty Cuthbert, Shirley Strickland, Murray Rose and Dawn Fraser dominated their events and television, introduced in Australia in time to broadcast the events, made sure their success became part of Australian sporting history.

Ron Clarke lights the Olympic Flame of the 1956 Summer Olympic Games

Photo by News Ltd/Newspix

Penpals would write to each other, sometimes from interstate or overseas

Shutterstock

Did you have a penpal?

Before Facebook, Twitter and texting, perfect strangers would write to each other as penpals.

I never had a penpal, but I remember my elder sister developed a long-lasting relationship through a penpal scheme with a girl in England and stayed in touch right up until recent times. I also had a friend who had a penpal in New York and eventually travelled to the US to meet and stay with her and her family.

From memory, there were penpal programs, where you could select a name and address and write a letter and they would reply. It was to foster international relations and it helped kids learn to express themselves in the written word.

I don't know if there are still penpal schemes operating, I suspect not, as it would seem so slow nowadays when you can reach someone on the other side of the world instantly.

Did you have a penpal as you were growing up?

#9
FACT

Vines first arrived in Australia along with the First Fleet in 1788, and vineyards were established near Parramatta and Camden in the early 1800s. However, wine production didn't really take off until 1828, when the first commercial region was established in the Hunter Valley. With help from Italians, Swiss and Germans most states were producing and exporting wine as early as the mid-1850s.

Playing records was a great way to catch up

Photo by Ted Holliday/Newspix

How easy do kids have it these days? With all the very latest songs available for immediate download from iTunes within hours of being released, or words to any song ever recorded now available instantly on Google.

Gone are the days when you would hear a song on the radio, head off to the local record shop to buy it, only to discover it was a brand new recording and not available in Australia yet, order it, wait weeks for it to arrive and when it finally landed, take it home and play it over and over and over again on the radiogram or record player.

Portable record players started to emerge in the early 1960s. By then the transistor revolution meant that records could be played on a battery powered portable device, which meant you could play records anywhere, anytime.

As teenagers we'd often get together on a Saturday night to listen to our friend's new records, swap ideas and talk about music.

It all seems so tame now, but back then it was a great night out with friends.

It was one of the greatest peacetime naval disasters in Australia's maritime history.

On 10 February 1964, two Australian warships, aircraft carrier HMAS *Melbourne* and the destroyer HMAS *Voyager* were engaged in manoeuvres off Jervis Bay. During the course of the exercises *Melbourne* collided into *Voyager* – the aircraft carrier's bow striking just behind the bridge and cutting the destroyer in two.

Eighty-two men were killed aboard the destroyer. Most were killed immediately.

Some were trapped in the bow section, which sank within 10 minutes. Although the *Melbourne* was also severely damaged there were no fatalities and it was able to sail back to Sydney the next morning carrying survivors of the *Voyager*.

Following two Royal Commissions into the collision, while the inattentiveness of the lookouts and bridge crew on board the *Voyager* were found to be major contributing factors, the exact cause of the accident has, officially, been difficult to determine.

HMAS *Melbourne*

Photo by News Ltd/Newspix

1966

Condemned as racist, the Golliwog symbol has been removed from public life

Museum Victoria. Reg. No: SH 000017

It's fascinating how things change over time ... For example, back in the '60s it was nothing for Mum to have some Arnott's Golliwog biscuits in the biscuit barrel for hungry kids after school.

Golliwog biscuits were first sold in the 1960s, and were made in the shape of the Golliwog toy, which was popular at that time. The name was changed to Scalliwag in the mid-1990s. However, the biscuits remained in the shape of a Golliwog and the product was discontinued by the late 1990s. Golliwogs went out of favour around the world in all kinds of commercial areas, from toys to children's books to foodstuffs, as they have been perceived as being inherently racist.

'The Lanky Yank', Don Lane hosted several different versions of the 'Tonight Show' over the period 1965 to 1983

Wikipedia

Don Lane first appeared on our TV screens in 1965 after fellow comedian Dave Allen was sacked from his 'Tonight Show' by TCN 9 in Sydney. Lane was originally hired to fill the spot for six weeks, but by the end of the fourth week the original contract was extended to forty weeks.

He was a natural-born entertainer and delighted the Sydney TV audiences with his comedy sketches, interviews and good-natured banter. The show continued with successful ratings until 1969 when Don decided to return to the US to perform in Las Vegas where he also appeared on 'The Sonny and Cher Comedy Hour'.

He came back to Australia to perform in a benefit concert for the victims of Cyclone Tracy in 1975 and was hired to replace Ernie Sigley as the host of 'In Melbourne Tonight' after Sigley had publicly criticised Kerry Packer on air.

This time Lane was teamed up with Bert Newton and although the two had never worked together before, there was an immediate on-screen chemistry. They went on to produce some of the finest live television ever produced and were 'must' viewing for over 30% of the national TV audience.

Because of budget restrictions introduced by Channel 9 in 1983, the show was axed, despite its healthy ratings. 'The Don Lane Show' ended on 13 November 1983, Lane's 50th birthday. His final episode ran for two and a half hours and ended with an emotional performance of Peter Allen's 'Once Before I Go'. He then took a final bow with 'The Don Lane Show' written in lights behind him and the screen faded to black.

Having fun in the backyard on the Hills Hoist

Fairfax Syndication

Australia has created some of the most famous items and produced some the best sporting people on earth.

The Hills Hoist is up there with them! Adelaide is the home and producer of this world-famous invention.

Remember before the Hills Hoist came along in the '50s we had clothes lines that stretched across the back yard and had to be propped up on wash day.

Lance Hill began to manufacture the Hills rotary clothes hoist in his backyard in Adelaide back in 1945. His wife apparently wanted an inexpensive replacement to the line and prop she had for drying clothes. It took a few years but eventually every back yard would have a Hills Hoist, not only in Adelaide but in countless countries right around the world!

Who can remember swinging on the 'Hoist' and making it their merry go round? Wet clothes and all!

'Read all about it ...' Paper boy sells the *Telegraph* on a busy Brisbane street

Photo by News Ltd/Newspix

Paper boys and girls were such an important part of our lives right up until they disappeared from the street corners in the early '80s. Remember finishing work around 5 or 5.30pm, rushing to catch the bus, tram or train, and the paper seller would be there, standing with a big stack of the latest edition of the afternoon paper: 'Newsssspaper ... Latest red spot edition ... Get your latest news heeeyah!!'

Back then, journalists wrote the stories, the advertising department sold the ads, newsagents and paper boys sold the papers on street corners.

These days it's much more complicated with newspapers now an on-line product, where news is updated every few minutes, people download the paper onto their iPad or tablet to read on the train or bus. I often think about how much simpler life was before the advent of the computer, when the paper was sold on the street corner.

As a child growing up in suburbia in the '50s, '60s and '70s, I used to go outside and sit on the front veranda to catch the cool breeze on a hot summer's night when the sun went down.

There was no air conditioning, or even electric fans, back then and if we couldn't go to the beach (because it was a school night), Dad would turn on the sprinklers on the lawn and we'd run under the shower of water to get wet and cool down. I also remember my father hosing down the walls of our brick house to try and cool it down.

If it stayed stinking hot on some nights we'd even sleep outside on the lawn, under the stars, without fear of being molested or murdered. Occasionally we'd sleep at the beach, once again without fear, and be treated to a bottle of lemonade, or an ice cream, which in those times was such a special treat.

What are some of your special memories of growing up in Australia during those years?

Gerald Brockelsby jumping over the sprinkler in the back garden of his family home at Blackburn in 1953. Children often played in the sprinkler in the backyard to escape from summer heat

Museum Victoria. Reg. No: MM 110316.

#10
FACT

Two million people sought to leave Vietnam after the communist victory in 1975. Although we talk about 'boat people', of the 94 000 Indochinese who arrived in Australia, only 2000 came by boat. Suburbs across our cities were transformed with less upheaval than anyone could have expected, given that there'd been so little migration from Asia to Australia until then.

Do the youth of today still consider car ownership in the same way as we Baby Boomers did?

When I was a teenager in the early '60s, owning a car was more than just having a means of transport. It was freedom, independence, and a rite-of-passage into adulthood. It was my boyhood dream, to own my own car!

Owning a car was a rite of passage in my day
Photo by Ray Saunders/Newspix

A car to the teenage Baby-Boomer generation represented so much about growing up, about standing on your own two feet. We loved our cars, it was an extension of who we were!

According to a recent survey, 46% of today's teenagers would choose internet access, or having a mobile phone, over owning a car.

I vividly remember my first car, a 1949 Austin A40, which cost me £150. Sixty MPH flat as a tack and with the big ends knocking, yet I remember it with great affection.

'The Twist' craze hit Australia in 1960 when the song was a national smash hit for American performer, Chubby Checker.

Chubby once described the dance moves 'like putting out a cigarette with both feet and coming out of a shower and wiping your bottom with a towel to the beat'.

It was the dance craze that spanned the generation gap between young and old

because anybody could do it.

It came as something of a shock for teenagers and youngsters of the day to see their parents dancing to a song that they also danced to.

Dancing the Twist, 1962

Photo by News Ltd/Newspix

Right through to the 1950s many backyards had
home-made bomb shelters

Courtesy of Kym Prime

Kym Prime shared this photo from the family album, which might bring back a few childhood memories for some:

This photo from the late 1940s is of my grandparents backyard in suburban Adelaide. The sloping structure leads to a bomb shelter built by my grandfather during the war.

There were quite a number of home-made air-raid shelters built in suburban backyards in the '40s, which survived well into the '50s. My wife often reminisces about a neighbour's backyard, which had a bomb shelter built by the owner in preparation for a Japanese air attack.

I vividly recall as a child all the old forts and guns scattered around coastal suburbs and towns, all built in case of a foreign invasion.

Bob Hawke celebrates the America's Cup victory

Photo by News Ltd/Newspix

Remember the sheer excitement that gripped the whole nation when *Australia II* won the America's Cup back in 1983?

The US yacht *Liberty* won the first, second and fourth race, but *Australia II* took the third, and came back to win the fifth and sixth. This was the first time the America's Cup had needed a sixth race, and a seventh to decide the winner.

Liberty won the start by eight seconds and over the course of the race there were three lead changes, as each of the yachts tried to gain the advantage. On the final leg, *Australia II* passed *Liberty* and crossed the finish line with a winning margin of a mere 41 seconds, becoming the first successful challenger in 132 years.

Australia erupted into celebration and prompted our larrikin Prime Minister of the day, Bob Hawke, to declare on national TV that 'any boss who sacks anyone for not turning up for work today is a bum'.

What are your memories of that dramatic day in 1983?

#11
FACT

'Breaker Breaker.' There was a craze for CB radios (Citizen Band or short distance radios) in the 1970s. A little like the mobile phones of their day, CB radio was used especially by long-distance truck drivers who developed their own lingo, but many hobbyists used CB radios too. By 1978 there were 750 registered CB radio clubs across Australia.

Remember when Mum would take you to buy a new pair of school shoes, take them home and give them to Dad who would carefully shape and glue on some hard wearing Dunlop soles and heels?

He would then tack on a steel toe and heel plate to give the shoes longer-lasting wear. I was watching a TV program last night, set back in the '50s, and when one of the characters removed his shoe it had the old steel-toe plate. I hadn't thought about it in years, but I started remembering how this was done to all our shoes, no doubt to save money.

Almost every home had a cast iron shoe last and long after all the kids shoes were done, the old shoe last ended up as a door stopper.

Do you remember your Dad fixing your shoes on the old shoe last?

Courtesy of Market Lavington Museum

77

The 'Young Talent Time' TV show was on Channel 10 on Saturday nights.

The original series ran from 1971 until 1988 and was hosted by Johnny Young. The show was revived in 2012 with very limited success.

The original YTT was a great show for the whole family and featured a core group of young performers (very similar to 'The Mickey Mouse Club'), and a weekly junior talent quest. The 'Young Talent Time' team performed popular songs along with the top-hit songs of the day.

The program launched the careers of a number of Australian performers, including Jamie Redfern, Tina Arena and Dannii Minogue, and spawned numerous hit singles, fifteen Young Talent Time albums, a film, swap cards, boardgames, toys, and numerous Logie awards.

At the time of writing, I believe Johnny Young is still working 'on air' in Perth and hosts a daily radio show.

Members of the Young Talent Time team, including Johnny Young and (*on his left*) Tina Arena

Photo by News Ltd/Newspix

Hanging out the washing after the weekly wash

Photo by News Ltd/Newspix

Monday was always 'wash day' at our place.

I remember Mum using an old copper while the cement laundry troughs were part and parcel of every wash house, along with a hand-operated wringer.

The wash house (not called a laundry back then) was usually separate from the house and quite often the water was not laid on. That meant the copper and wash troughs had to be filled by carting buckets of water from the rain-water tank or outside tap.

Mum would be up early and Dad would have set the fire ready to boil the copper. Once the water was boiling, the whites would go in first, allowed to boil before being taken out with a long wooden stick and placed into one of the double cement troughs. There was also the 'blue-ing' process, blue blocks inside small material sacks (Reckitt's Blue) and then put through the wringer.

The Pope washing machine came along a little later, which had an electric wringer and made things a lot easier.

Comic Court wins the Melbourne Cup, 1950

Photo by News Ltd/Newspix

Can you remember the first time you heard about the Melbourne Cup?

I say *heard* because of course most of us would not have seen a Melbourne Cup until TV first arrived in Australia in the late 1950s.

The first Cup I recall was in 1950, I would have been in Grade 2 at school, and the

teacher turned on the radio so the whole class of 6 year olds could hear 'Australia's Greatest Race'.

Strangely enough, I've never forgotten that moment.

It really is the 'race that stops a nation' and every year on that first Tuesday in November, we would all down tools for at least a few minutes to listen to the big race.

Cup Day is a public holiday in Melbourne and some parts of country Victoria, and although not a declared holiday in other states, many people take the day off work or 'pull a sickie'.

Delivery vans brought all sorts of products to our home , including bread, milk, groceries, blocks of ice for the ice chest and miracle ointments

State Library of New South Wales, PXA 978/1-100

Before it was common for a family to have a car, delivery vans brought groceries to the home. Back then the choice in milk was simply the number of pints ladled by the milkman into the billy early each morning, later replaced by glass bottles.

Bread was often delivered by horse and cart, and the greengrocer would fill an order from a large green van. Men used special tongs to carry huge, dripping blocks of ice down the gravel drive to the ice chest in the kitchen and the Rawleigh's man called with his big case in which he carried everything from miracle ointments to hair ribbons.

The rabbittoh came on Friday afternoons and the tinker who sharpened all the knives and the scissors called about once a year.

What memories do you have of home deliveries from your own childhood years?

#12
FACT

Australian children's television has had so many much-loved animal characters (inhabited by humans) who don't speak, notably Humphrey B. Bear and Fat Cat, who had his own long-running show, 'Fat Cat and Friends'. Ossie Ostrich often found it hard to stop speaking on the other hand, and of course we had B1 and B2, talking bananas who wore pyjamas too.

Jack Jones and his wife working in their butcher shop

Peter Jones Collection, NT Library

Here's a photo to get you remembering back to the days of a visit to the old local butcher shop.

Mum would ask for hoggett (don't think we could afford lamb) and sausages and the butcher would cut off a generous slice of fritz (devon) or a bit of raw sausage for us kids, standing waiting patiently, making swirly patterns with the sawdust on the floor.

The butcher always had his knife sharpener at the ready, or a meat cleaver on his big chopping block and an electric saw to cut the joints while you were there in the shop. He'd wrap things like liver, kidneys and hearts in butcher's paper and yesterday's newspaper.

Note all the cuts of meat hanging unrefrigerated on the meat racks.

Very different to the sanitised sparkling butcher shops of today, or the supermarkets where everything is pre-wrapped in plastic.

Poseidon shares trading strongly

Photo by News Ltd/Newspix

In 1969 Poseidon shares were suddenly the rage and on everybody's lips. I had several friends who made an enormous amount of money almost overnight when they 'got in' on the share-market boom.

In 1969, it was reported that a prospector with Poseidon Limited had discovered nickel deposits at Mt Windarra in Western Australia and pegged some 40 claims in the area for the company.

Nickel worldwide was in high demand at the time and the discoveries created news headlines and generated one of the largest mineral booms the Australian Stock Exchange had ever seen.

In the five months, from September 1969 to February 1970, Poseidon's shares sky-rocketed from $1.85 to an incredible $280 per share. But as the old saying goes, 'what goes up' ... So the boom didn't last long and there were people who purchased shares at the top price and lost all their money.

HAIR

The thing that springs to mind about *Hair*, the stage musical, is the big nude scene at the end. I believe it was a first in Australia.

The local production of *Hair* opened in Sydney on 4 June 1969 at the Metro Theatre in Kings Cross. It was well-reviewed, despite the bomb scare and resultant evacuation. It was a major social event. Many well-known local celebrities attended.

Hair was a major success with audiences, breaking local box office

Hair was the rock musical that arrived in Australia in 1969 and created a storm of controversy because of the big nude scene

Photo by News Ltd/Newspix

records, and generating enormous media interest because of its then-controversial stand against the Vietnam War, the nudity and the music. It ran for nearly two years in Sydney before shifting to Melbourne, premiering there on 8 June 1971 – it then went on a national tour.

Playing in the school orchestra, a tambourine, a triangle, a cymbal or the drum!

ARW

Do you recall playing in the school orchestra as a child?

If you did, this photo will take you back to those years at primary school when the music teacher would gather a group of poor unsuspecting kids to form an orchestra for the end-of-year concert. From memory at our school, you could get out of PE if you were selected to play an instrument.

This photo was taken probably from the mid-late 1950s. The pianist was either the music teacher at school, or possibly a school volunteer, while the kids are playing cymbals, drums, triangles, etc.

#13
FACT

'Looking great in Cylinders, out in the sea ... You can turn your back on the world.' Remember Crystal Cylinders, the Australian surfwear brand with the wavy 'CC' logo and the sun-burnished surfer boys and girls in the TV ads? The trademark is now owned by a Sydney clothing company, so we may yet see it on labels again one day.

In the photo I love the little boy standing right behind the music teacher. He was either not exactly happy to be involved or was concentrating so hard he forgot to smile!

Great photo of years long gone, but not forgotten.

Ian Williams shared this photo:

This is a part of my collection. BEX has reached iconic status these days and hence, very collectable … There is big money in nostalgia, and it shows no signs of slowing.

Thanks Ian … Who would have thought that Bex would be a collectable item after all that bad press!

I remember my mother and grandmother took Bex, but I don't believe they were addicted as some people were.

The product was sold as a sort of pick-me-up or something to calm you down and get through the rough parts of the day.

A Bex, a cup of tea and a good lie down would fix almost anything.

'A Bex, a cup of tea and a good lie down would fix almost anything'

Courtesy of Ian Williams

After the Sunday roast was prepared and in the stove, Mum and the girls would make a cake and biscuits for the coming week

Photo by News Ltd/Newspix

Every Sunday after church it was a tradition, in both summer and winter, to have a roast dinner with all the trimmings.

The wood was cut the night before and the stove was lit after church on Sunday morning. The meat was usually hogget and vegies, including potatoes, pumpkin, shelled peas and Brussels sprouts – they were usually from Dad's own vegetable garden in the backyard.

The meat and veg were all cooked in dripping and roasted until golden brown, even the Brussels sprouts tasted good!

After the roast was on and in the stove, Mum and the girls (my sisters) would make a cake (one of Mum's famous sponges) and several batches of biscuits to last the family for the week ahead.

Children looking hopefully at toys!

Photos by Fred Carew/Newspix

Long before stores such as ToysRUs and Toyworld there were very few shops that sold toys for 365 days of the year.

Most of our serious toy shopping was done at Christmas and then it was mainly 'window shopping', so we could tell Father Christmas just exactly what we wanted him to leave.

I am amazed at the number of toys, games, devices, gadgets and gizmos that my grandchildren have already, and continue to receive. They play with a lot of them and some are very sophisticated, including a robotic dog that is programmed through constant use.

As a little boy, I would have had about six small toy cars in my collection; my grandson (aged 8) would probably have about 200. His little sister (aged 6) would have maybe 100 dolls of various shapes and sizes. My sisters would have had maybe 10 between the three of them.

We live in very different times now. When we were growing up in the '50s and '60s there was usually just the one income and very little spare money, especially for luxuries like children's toys.

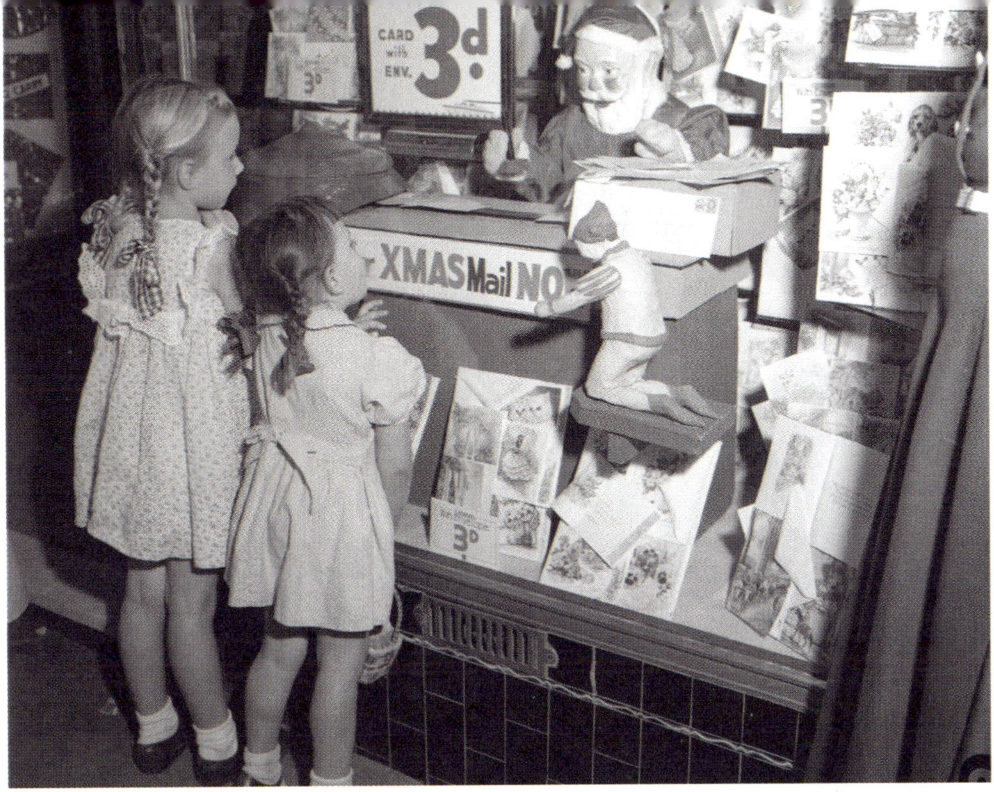
CARD with ENV.
3d
XMAS Mail NO
3D

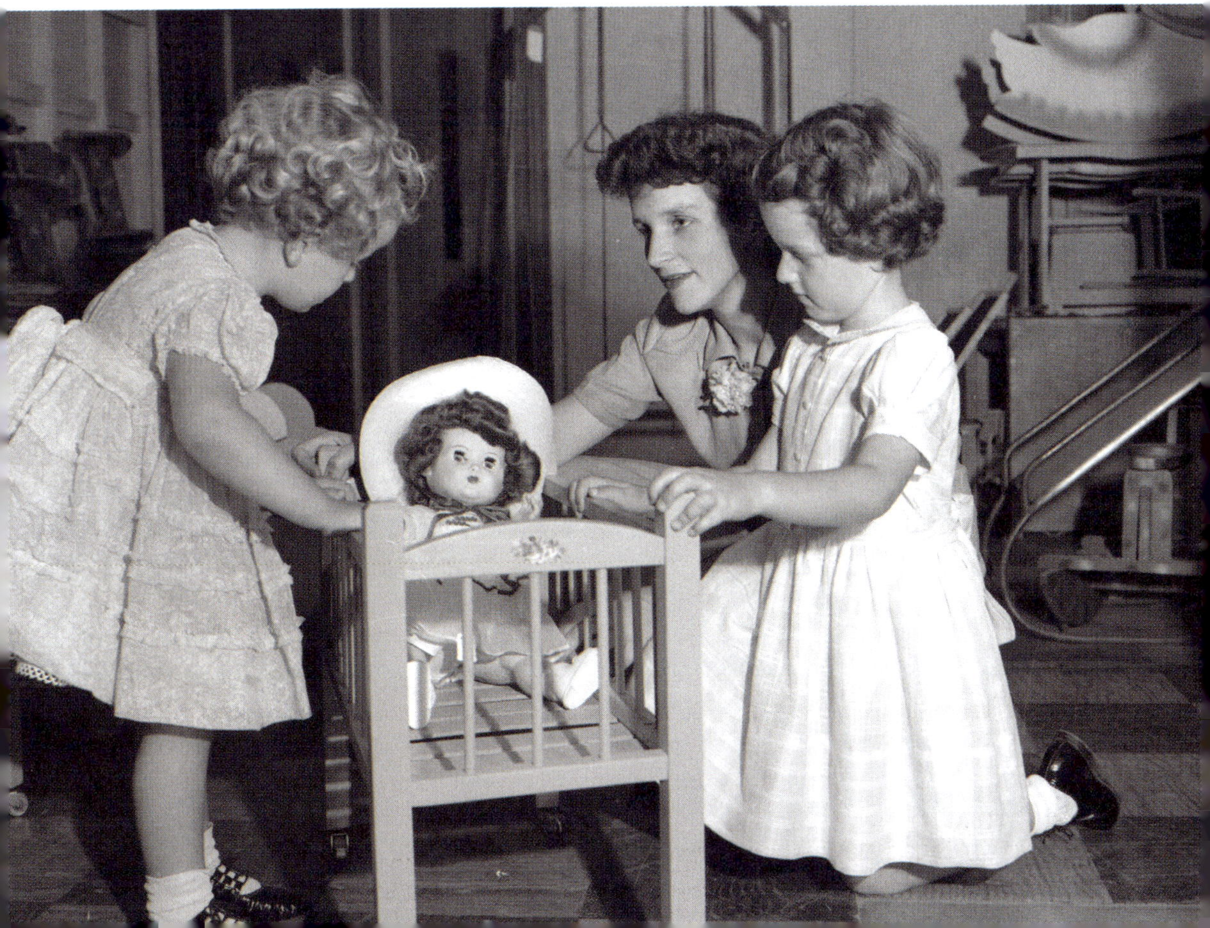

Remember 'lamington drives' at school when all the Mums would gather in the school hall and make hundreds of lamingtons to sell as a fundraiser for the school?

Courtesy of Women's Weekly

Mandy Whitrod shared her memories about lamington drives:

> I was in the middle of making some lamingtons today and thought about the good old lamington drives we used to do for fundraisers ... slabs of home-made cake, pots of chocolate sauce and elbow deep in coconut with lines of women taking part. Not like today where a lamington drive means taking orders for a bakery delivery. I think they've become a thing of the past.

Mandy also included comments from a *Women's Weekly* magazine article from 1982, about lamington drives: 'What is the richest cake in the world? Unquestionably, from a money-making point of view, it has to be the little Aussie lamington.'

Were you ever involved in a lamington drive for the school?

#14
FACT

Have you seen *Number 11, 1952,* also known as *Blue Poles?* Purchased amid controversy by the National Gallery of Australia in 1973, Jackson Pollock's abstract expressionist painting remains one of the gallery's major paintings. The $1.3 million price tag prevented the gallery's director, James Mollison from purchasing it without the authorisation of Prime Minister Gough Whitlam and is now valued between $20–$100 million.

Scanlen's Bubblegum produced a range of cards and stickers for kids to collect

Courtesy of Robert Verrall

When we were kids growing up from the '50s to the '80s we used to be great collectors of cards and stickers.

Shell service stations published collector cards and there were a number of different sets, including footballers and Australian scenes. Coca-Cola soft drink bottle tops had images of pop stars, TV station personalities or footy players underneath the cork seal. Once collected the caps were glued on to a cardboard folder.

Weet-Bix collector cards offered a range of different series, and Redhead match box labels also had a number of different collections available over the years. Scanlen's Bubblegum collector cards offered different sets, one that comes to mind was the 1960s 'Batman' television program characters.

Robert Verrall posted a photo of his Scanlens Cricket Sticker Album and Ian Keith Kershaw reminded me that MacRobertson's chocolates had collectable wrappers like this one of Cliff Richard and the Shadows from the early '60s.

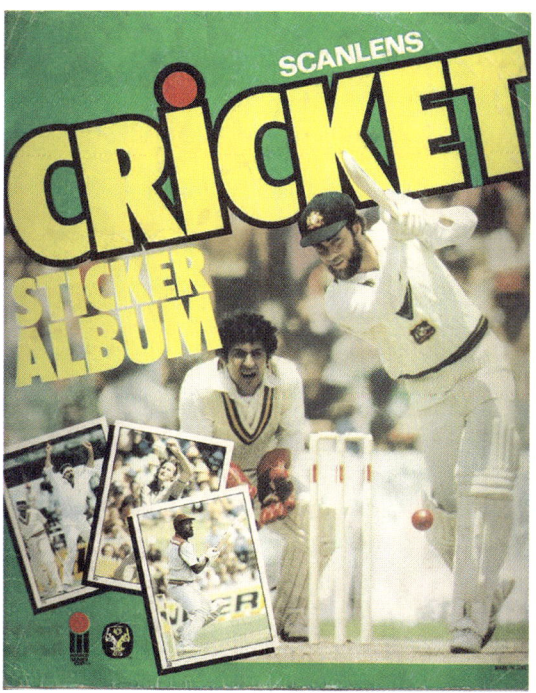

'MacRobertson's chocolates used to have collectable wrappers, an example of which was on a small chocolate bar. This one has Cliff Richard and the Shadows from the early sixties!' – Ian Keith Kershaw

Courtesy of Anvers Chocolates

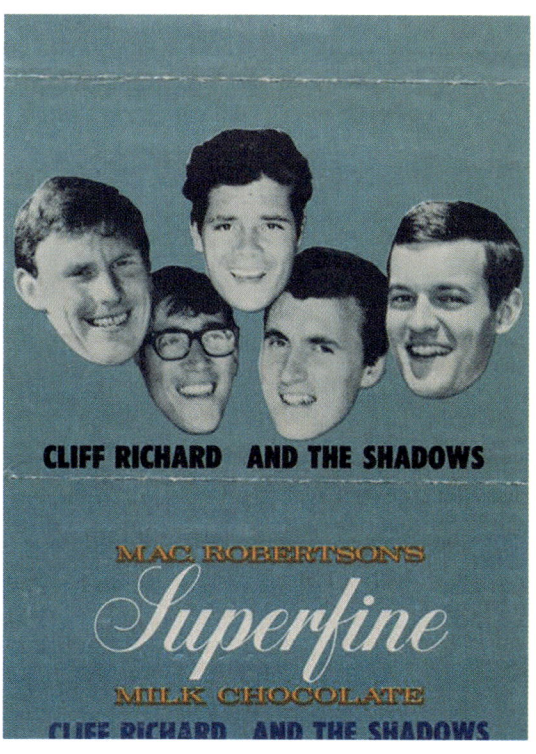

Mel Gibson and Bruce Spence in *Mad Max*

Photo by News Ltd/Newspix

The first of the *Mad Max* movies, with Australian actor Mel Gibson, was released in November 1979.

The film is set in a futuristic Australia where, due to an energy crisis, society has begun to break down with motorcycle gangs terrorising people and riding roughshod over the law.

Enter 'Mad Max' (Mel Gibson), a sort of law enforcer, who takes on the baddies using their own rules and tactics to teach them a few lessons.

The film did extremely well at the box office. It held the Guinness world record for most profitable film for decades, and has been credited with helping to open up the global market to Australian films at the time.

Due to its success *Mad Max* became the first in a series, with sequels *Mad Max 2: The Road Warrior* in 1981 and *Mad Max Beyond Thunderdome* in 1985.

Brian Edwards posted a question on the Australia Remember When Facebook website:

> Before she married my Dad in the '40s, my late Mum was a comptometer operator at 'The Glass Factory'. Can you please tell me anything about either of these things? Thank you, Brian.

In the days prior to calculators, large companies such as banks, insurance companies and private corporations, hired people to run adding machines all day, checking the figures that would be entered in the General Ledger.

The adding machines were called comptometers and the job entailed adding up figures, processing invoices and acting as a corporate version of a cash register. After World War II, young women would have been given this kind of clerical work in computing sums and processing invoices.

Apparently the noise in the place was phenomenal, the clickity clack of those machines was incredible. The job required enormous concentration and wasn't well paid. Comptometers were eventually phased out after computers and other more efficient technologies came along, which helped companies keep more accurate records and process their invoices. Another job that no longer exists.

A comptometrist at work

Photo by News Ltd/Newspix

Despite resembling the feathers of an emu, this large chunk of debris is actually from the American satellite, *Skylab*. Remember it falling from the sky on 11 July 1979? NASA had decided to decommission *Skylab* as it was old and not functioning effectively anymore. The plan was to send it into a controlled tumble over the Pacific Ocean so that it would break apart on entering Earth's atmosphere, and any debris would safely fall on open water. Not going exactly as planned, some of the debris landed on populated areas of Western Australia, much of it falling near Esperance. After the initial shock subsided, authorities decided to give some of the debris a supporting role, appropriately enough, at the Miss Universe competition held just four days later in Perth. It's questionable whether the idea was a success as the piece in this picture is a bit too ugly to make an appearance at a beauty competition!

One of *Skylab*'s cylindrical oxygen tanks in a supporting role at Miss Universe, 1979

National Archives of Australia, A6135, K19/7/79/2

A 1950s cash register. Some of the early cash registers required the operator to do a lot of mental arithmetic to work out the change

dreamstime

Before we had computerised checkouts, there were cash registers!

According to Wikipedia, the cash register was first invented in 1879. Early registers were entirely mechanical, without receipts. The employee was required to ring up every transaction on the register, and when the total key was pushed, the drawer opened and a bell would ring, alerting the manager to a sale taking place. Those original machines were nothing but simple adding machines.

More complicated and versatile versions were invented over time until today, where we have computers that can now weigh, compute and accurately charge your supermarket purchases at a self-checkout.

When I see these cash registers I'm always reminded of going shopping with my mother, before checkouts, when people served customers from behind a counter, added up the total on a cash register and calculated the change themselves. I wonder how many shop assistants would be able to calculate change today?

The 'tennis twins', Lew Hoad and Ken Rosewall.
Throughout the '50s we would listen to the
wireless as they played in the Davis Cup

*Argus Newspaper Collection of Photographs, State
Library of Victoria, H2004.100/1584*

Remember when the Davis Cup was the biggest tennis event of the year?

I recall in the mid-50s how the whole family would be glued to the wireless for the three days after Christmas, in the summer heat, listening to the 'tennis twins', Lew Hoad and Ken Rosewall, playing for Australia, mostly against the Americans, in the Davis Cup.

They were called twins, but were nothing alike. Hoad was blonde with a powerful build, while Rosewall had dark hair, was short and thin but the two boys could play tennis.

All along the street, the front doors would be wide open to try and catch a bit of a breeze (no such thing as air conditioning then), and you could hear that everyone was listening to the same program on the ABC, a ball-by-ball commentary on the games. It was almost as big a sporting event as the Melbourne Cup at the time.

Remember staying up on Good Friday night for the all-night horror movie marathons with Deadly Earnest on Channel 0/10?

Deadly Earnest originated in Perth on Channel 7 sometime in the early–mid '60s with Roland Barnes and was revived in Sydney by Ian Bannerman in 1966. The idea was apparently so successful that local variants soon turned up in Melbourne, Brisbane and Adelaide. Melbourne's Deadly Earnest was Ralph Baker on ATV-0, Hedley Cullen played the character in Adelaide on SAS-10, Shane Porteus (from a 'Country Practice') on Brisbane TVQ-0 and Ian Bannerman in Sydney on TEN-10.

TV was black and white back then and the movies were usually B-grade horror films, but it was always such a treat to be able to stay up all night and watch TV with family or friends. Most people look back now and remember the Deadly Earnest movies and the marathons with great affection.

Photos (*from top left*) Ian Bannerman (Sydney), Ralph Baker (Melbourne) and Hedley Cullen (Adelaide) and Shane Porteus (Brisbane)

Courtesy of National Film and Sound Archive

Each of us has memories of childhood holidays. They generally include long road trips, sometimes with a caravan in tow, and the only entertainment provided by Mum, usually seated in the front seat next to Dad as he drove the car on to the destination.

Unlike today where kids can choose from a plethora of digital games and gadgets, we filled the time playing games such as 'Spotto', 'I Spy With My Little Eye' and 'Riddle-me Riddle-me Ree.'

There were lots of arguments between siblings about who was taking up too much space, and inevitably all the kids joined in the chorus to ask repeatedly, 'Are we there yet? ... Are we there yet?'

There were no seat-belt regulations then and the only air conditioning on a 40+ degree day was to wind down the four windows to let the hot air flow through the car.

So much has changed now with the family touring holiday. Cars are bigger,

more comfortable and fitted with all the latest safety equipment, seat belts for all, air conditioning, and some even have individual DVD screens for the children in the back seats. There are also iPads and iPhones, tablets or hand-held mini-computers on which to watch movies, play games and listen to music.

There is so much for the kids to do while travelling in the back seat now.

And yet, I think, I still hear the chorus 'Are we there yet? ... Are we there yet?'

'Are we there yet? ... Are we there yet?'
Photo by News Ltd/Newspix

#15
FACT

Ken Done's designs are well-known to Australians, especially during the '80s when he established a design company 'Done Art and Design' with his wife Judy. His highly colourful designs could be seen splashed everywhere – from boardies to dinner plates. Despite his huge commercial success, Done is a serious painter and has staged numerous solo exhibitions worldwide.

The Commodore 64 was my second computer. I'd originally started with an Atari, but the Commodore was a big step up from there

Wikipedia, photo Bill Bertram

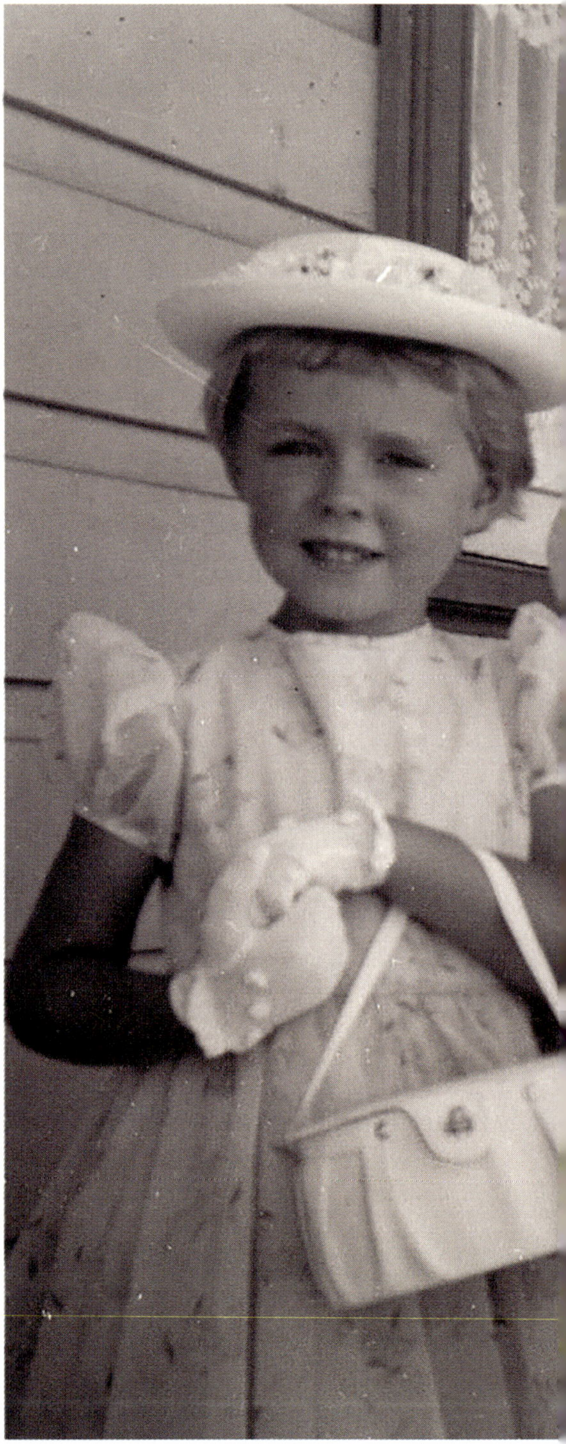

What was your first computer?

Remember your first venture into the digital world? It was probably with a Commodore 64. Although these days it looks like an unimpessive keyboard-like box, the Commodore C64 was incredibly popular.

It was first released in 1982 and more C64s have been sold than any other single computer system, even to this day. That's about 17 million systems, according to the Commodore 1993 Annual Report.

It seems amazing when you look around today at the impressive array of desktop computers, lap tops, tablets and smart phones that just over 30 years ago, very few people had anything to do with computers.

There was a time when people always dressed in their 'Sunday best' whenever they 'went to town'.

Looking back at old photos, taken during the late '50s and '60s, the thing that strikes me is how well dressed everybody was, especially compared to today. I recall as a child, when my mother would go to town she always wore her Sunday best dress, including hat and gloves. That was in the '50s, but people still continued to dress well and men wore a suit and tie and women wore their best dresses if going to the city to shop or going out on a Saturday night right through the '60s and early '70s.

I was walking through the city on my lunch break recently and I saw two men in smart suits but not one woman in a hat and gloves. I spotted mostly very casual attire and jeans, in some cases torn and dirty jeans, and other assorted clothing, some of which would probably not have been worn to do the gardening in the '50s and '60s.

'This is my sister and me about to catch the bus to town with Mum in 1960. Lovely memory'

Courtesy of Denise Trent

It's fun to remember the past, but there was also a dark side to the 'good old days'.

In the '50s, Australia had a polio epidemic that left many children, and some adults too, crippled for life. There was widespread fear across the nation each time another outbreak of the disease occurred. Thousands of children spent months in special isolation wards, unable to breathe outside the 'iron lungs' that kept them alive. It was not uncommon that in almost every community, children were affected and would suddenly disappear from school or the playground.

The first glimmer of hope for preventing the spread of polio appeared in Australia in 1954 when it was reported that a new vaccine was being tested on people for the first time. The vaccine was eventually proven

Many young children were affected by polio in the 1950s. I remember how my grandmother made us wear 'camphor' bags around our necks at all times

State Library of South Australia, B49040

to be effective and in 1956 the Australian Government launched a mass immunisation program for the prevention of poliomyelitis. All school children and pre-school children were immunised as part of the campaign.

I have vivid recollections of lining up at school, with all my classmates, to get a 'needle' and trying to be brave and show no fear. While most of us treasure the memories of our childhood, the polio epidemic of the 1950s casts a dark shadow over the decade and its legacy was devastating for many families.

These are now called 'chatterboxes' and are apparently still popular at school. We made them all the time when we were kids

ARW

Oh the games we used to make up at school! We would take a sheet of paper, fold it over several times, write four colours on the exterior, odd and even numbers on the next layer and when those sections were lifted there was a message inside. Can you remember playing this game? I never knew it had a name but kids these days call them 'chatterboxes' and still play with them.

It was generally to do with telling the future and I always thought it was quite a neat little game. Did you make chatterboxes too?

A classic 'Loyal Royal' typewriter

dreamstime

Who learned to touch type at school?

'Now is the time for all good men to come to the aid of their party' and 'The quick brown fox jumps over the lazy dog'.

Unfortunately I never learned typing at school because I was a boy. Back in the day the girls in our class, and the girls in the whole school for that matter, were taught how to cook and sew, learnt shorthand and typing, while the boys got stuck with woodwork and sheet metal work.

I was a complete dunce at woodwork but I sure could have used those typing skills in my media career later. Not to mention cooking and sewing skills, which everyone needs at some time during their lives.

Most of our drive-in theatres have disappeared now, but in the '50s and '60s going to the drive-in was a very popular pastime.

The very first drive-in picture theatre opened in Burwood, Victoria, in 1954 and on opening night, was so popular, it caused traffic jams all along the highway. The other states soon followed when the Blue-Line drive-in located in Adelaide opened later

Burwood Drive-in, Melbourne

Photo by News Ltd/Newspix

that same year, followed by WA in 1955.

Sydney got its first taste of drive-in theatres when the Skyline Drive-ins at Frenchs Forest and Dundas were opened simultaneously in 1956.

When TV arrived in the latter part of the '50s, the drive-ins started to suffer a drop in numbers and over time, gradually closed down, the land being used for housing, shopping centres and the like.

I can't remember the last time I went to a drive-in, would've been a long time ago, but I recall the fun we had as kids and teenagers when we'd all pile in the car (and one in the boot) and head off to the local drive-in pictures.

#16
FACT

In 1969, *Hair* premiered in Sydney's Kings Cross. There was only one hitch: a bomb scare and mini-evacuation on opening night! Nonetheless, Australia was hooked. *Hair* 'sprouted' a new era of musical theatre. Who could forget *Jesus Christ Superstar* and the *Rocky Horror Picture Show*?

Once upon a time, air travel was seen as glamorous and exciting.

International flights were novel, and even on domestic routes, passengers often dressed to the nines, very different to the casual flight attire of today. Airline pilots were held in high-esteem and airline hostesses were considered to have one of the most exciting jobs in the world.

Most occupations on offer to young women back then were not particularly alluring. This is what gave being an air hostess such appeal.

Very few could resist the idea of a profession where you could travel, meet interesting people, and the designer uniform was the icing on the cake. Air hostesses were looked up to as movie stars, featured frequently in the newspaper social pages and magazines of the day and for several decades were a symbol of glamour and elegance.

TAA air hostesses – who also happened to be twins

Photo by Al Pascoe/Newspix

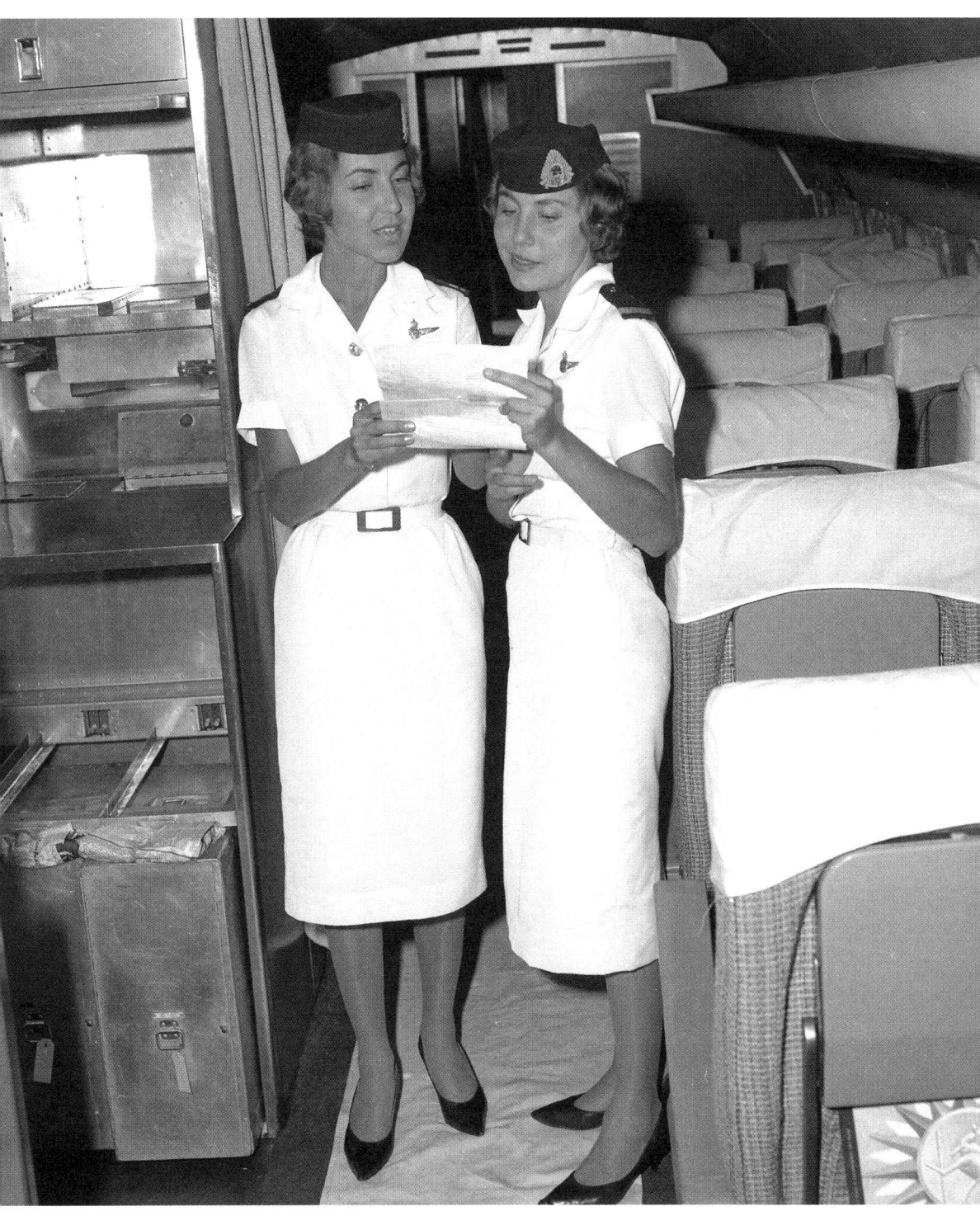

An original Sweetacres Jaffas' box, the packaging I remember from the 1960s

Courtesy of Steve Williams

We mostly took a cut lunch to school. Devon or fritz with sauce or sliced tomato, camp pie or cold cuts of lamb from the Sunday roast, or even just plain Vegemite or cheddar cheese sandwiches. But once a week there was tuck shop when we were allowed to buy pies, pasties or sausage rolls. There were also hot dogs, double-cut rolls, sandwiches, donuts and cream-filled

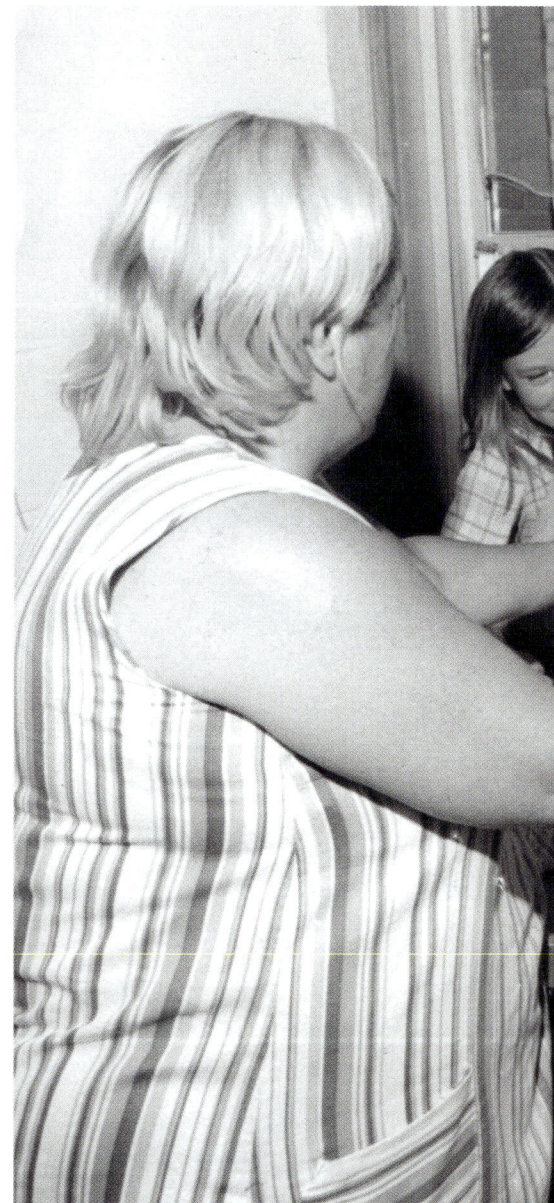

Seeing this image of an old Jaffas' box takes me right back to Saturday arvo at the flicks, when all the kids from the neighbourhood would go the matinee at the local picture theatre or fleapit.

There'd be a Randolph Scott and John Wayne picture on the same program, the weekly serial, a newsreel and a 'Heckle and Jeckle' cartoon. All the kids would boo when the hero kissed the girl and if the film broke (which it did regularly back then), complete pandemonium would ensue.

At interval we'd get a pass out and go to the shop a few doors down and buy some hot chips or a Chiko Roll, maybe some Fantales or a box of Jaffas. As most of the picture theatres had sloped wooden floors when one of the kids dropped his box of Jaffas, they would make a commotion as they all rolled down the slope. Some of the kids would start the Jaffas rolling and all the other kids would join in. Ahhh, fun memories!

buns. There were all sorts of lollies too, including conversation lollies, gobstoppers and licorice squares at four for a penny.

All the kids loved Tuckshop Day and occasionally there would be special fund-raising toffee days when all the Mums would make toffees in little patty pans, which would be sold at the tuck shop with all the funds raised going to the school.

Everybody was justifiably mad with excitement on Tuckshop Day!

Photo by News Ltd/Newspix

It's amazing to think that it's 40 years since the Tasman Bridge disaster, which tragically took the lives of 12 people. The disaster literally split Hobart in two and still haunts many Hobartians to this day. It was on the evening of 5 January 1975 when the bulk carrier, the *Lake Illawarra*, collided with pylons of the Tasman Bridge, taking out two of them and over 120 metres of the bridge decking. Seven of the ship's crew lost their lives as well as five car occupants who plunged 45 metres to their deaths after driving off the bridge. A number of other drivers and their passengers were extremely lucky to escape by jumping out of their cars as they teetered over the edge.

These car occupants were very lucky to live and tell the tale

Photo by News Ltd/Newspix

Shane Gould, our 'Golden Girl'

Photo by News Ltd/Newspix

Shane Gould was our 'Golden Girl' of 1972. At the age of just 15, Shane won five Olympic medals at the Munich Olympic Games. During her short career she was the holder of every freestyle world record from 100 metres to 1500 metres.

Twelve months after the games, Shane decided to retire. At the age of 19 she married Neil Innes and moved to the Margaret River area in Western Australia. They had four children before their marriage broke up during the 1990s.

2UE OFFICIAL TOP 40

as compiled from
The ORIGINAL and AUTHENTIC SURVEY of HIT TUNES

COMMENCING SATURDAY, APRIL 4

PUBLIC SURVEY *RECORD SALES* *MUSIC SALES* and a NATIONAL survey by the "BILLBOARD"

EIGHTY TOP 40 PREDICTIONS

MICK SIMMONS
BONDI JUNCTION
RECORDS-RADIO-GRAMOPHONES

		LAST WEEK	TIMES IN
1.	Smoke Gets in Your Eyes	1	10
2.	Gotta Travel On	10	6
3.	To Know Him is to Love Him	4	9
4.	Petite Fleur	2	6
5.	Venus	8	3
6.	Bimbombey	3	13
7.	Stagger Lee	5	6
8.	On the Street Where You Live	6	13
9.	Children's Marching Song	7	10
10.	All of a Sudden My Heart Sings	11	7
11.	Little Drummer Boy	20	6
12.	Bigger Than Texas	19	3
13.	Waltzing Matilda	16	4
14.	Beep Beep	9	13
15.	What Da Ya Know	12	6
16.	Sixteen Candles	21	4
17.	Blue Ribbon Baby	13	4
18.	With the Wind and the Rain in Your Hair	23	5

		LAST WEEK	TIMES IN
19.	Mardi Gras March	14	18
20.	The World Outside	17	10
21.	Come Prima	15	7
22.	All American Boy	18	6
23.	Donna	22	4
24.	Goodbye Baby	34	2
25.	Treasure of Your Love	25	3
26.	Don't Take Your Guns to Town	—	1
27.	She Say	32	4
28.	It's Only Make Believe	24	12
29.	Tomboy	33	2
30.	Ambrose (Part 5)	35	3
31.	Hey Sheriff	26	13
32.	Hawaiian Wedding Song	28	5
33.	Tall Paul	—	1
34.	I Got Stung	29	9
35.	I Got a Wife	—	1
36.	The Blob	37	4
37.	May You Always	31	5
38.	Tom Dooley	30	22
39.	Nola	38	2
40.	I Could Have Danced All Night	40	13

THESE DROPPED OUT:—

Pussy Cat	27	21
Problems	36	6
That Old Black Magic	39	10

Based on music sales record sales and disc jockey playings.

1. Yellow Bird
2. The Girl on Page 44
3. Pink Shoelaces
4. Plain Jane
5. Kiss Me Honey Honey Kiss Me
6. Wiggle Wiggle
7. Charlie Brown
8. Raspberries and Strawberries
9. I'm a Man
10. I Go Ape
11. Poor Boy
12. Move It
13. Little Space Girl
14. It Doesn't Matter Any More
15. I've Had It
16. I Cried a Tear
17. Blah Blah Blah (Yakety Yak)
18. Who Cares
19. Red River Rose
20. I'm Never Gonna Tell On You
21. Peter Gunn Theme
22. Please Mr. Sun
23. Because You're Young
24. Don't Pity Me
25. La Bamba
26. I'll Wait for You
27. Blue Hawaii
28. Pizza Boy U.S.A.
29. One Rose
30. Nobody But You
31. The Wedding
32. Morning Side of the Mountain
33. Are You Lonesome Tonight
34. Story of My Love
35. It's Just a Matter of Time
36. A House a Car and a Wedding Ring
37. That's Love
38. I've Got You Under My Skin
39. Love You Most of All
40. The Diary
41. My Happiness
42. Lonely Teardrops
43. Miss You
44. As Time Goes By
45. Apple Blossom Time
46. Sea Cruise
47. Tragedy
48. Where Were You
49. It's Only the Beginning
50. My Man
51. If I Didn't Care
52. Pretty Girls Everywhere
53. There Must Be a Way
54. Tiajuana Jail
55. Everybody Likes to Cha Cha
56. Happy Organ
57. Heavenly Lover
58. The Worryin' Kind
59. Trust in Me
60. Answer to a Maiden's

The first '2UE Official Top 40 Chart' was printed for distribution on 2 March 1958

eBay

Radio 2UE in Sydney was the first station in Australia to make their 'Top 40' chart available through various city and suburban record shops in 1958. Other radio stations in other cities soon followed.

I was an avid collector of the charts and religiously collected them from the late '50s until I got into radio in 1965. Most charts were never really an accurate reflection of record sales, but more a compilation of the music director's 'gut' feel, record company promotion, local band or performer's popularity and some sales figures.

Most radio stations stopped distributing their own 'charts' during the '80s when the record companies combined to present a more accurate chart, based purely on sales figures.

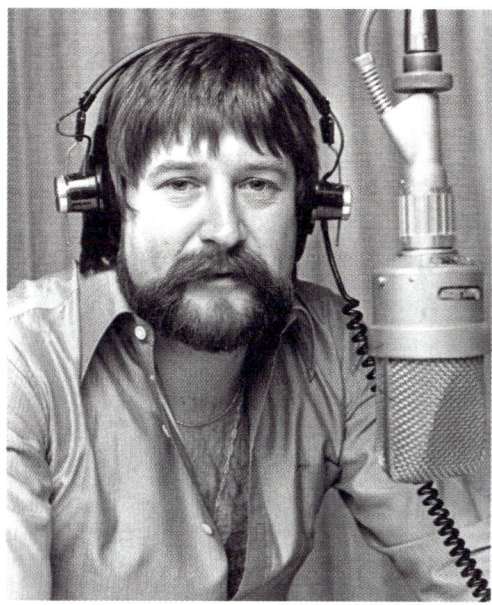

Derryn Hinch on air

Photo by News Ltd/Newspix

#17
FACT

If you grew up in the 1960s, 1970s or 1980s you would've owned – or at least had a friend who owned – a Mouse Trap board game, which first appeared in 1963. The torturous set-up was always worth it once that marble was rolling ... until it got stuck halfway down a ramp!

The Human Headline, Derryn Hinch, started his career in New Zealand as a newspaper reporter, later moving to Sydney and joining the afternoon paper, *The Sun*. His newspaper columns were often very controversial and he eventually found his way onto radio in Melbourne on talk station Radio 3AW.

He was often involved in on-air stunts, including being arrested live on radio, when he defied the government ban on discussing politics in the last two days leading up to a federal election.

Hinch became one of Australia's best-known broadcasters when he took a job with Channel 7 as compere of their national current affairs show.

He has remained a controversial character right throughout his long media career.

It wasn't just boys who wanted to own a cap gun

Courtesy of Kriss Sherwood

Kriss Sherwood shared a photo:

Annie Oakley was my hero so my Mum made me a beautiful costume and I wore it for a couple of years at least. However, I eventually learned that it was really Gail Davis the actor who I most admired. She could do all the tricks and stunts herself. In the opening credits she was riding her horse flat out, galloping while she was standing up, so effortlessly. I read all I could about her when I first had the internet, and also bought the full set of her TV series on DVD. All so great to watch again.

Toy gun, just like the one I had as a kid

State Library of South Australia, clrci15925961

The 1950s when boys were cowboys and played with toy guns

Courtesy of Ian Goed

During the '50s, '60s and '70s, 'Cowboys and Indians' and 'Cops and Robbers' were played, imitating the wireless serials, films and later television series.

Every young boy (and many a girl) aspired to owning a cap gun. It was a more innocent age and parents, or at least the majority, had no problems with this. After all, 'boys would be boys' and if they didn't have a toy gun, they would point a stick or worse make a slingshot or catapult, which were more lethal than the relatively mild 'pop' of a percussion cap.

I doubt you would be able to purchase a six gun in a shop these days, seen now as a symbol of violence. Yet at the same time youngsters are given an iPad or tablet where they can download violent video games, arm themselves with an AK47 and shoot and kill other players, complete with lots of blood.

Most Boomers I think would say that having a cap gun as a child did not influence their behaviour in later life.

Remember when in most big offices (and even some small ones) there was a tea lady with a trolley who brought a cup of tea, biscuits, a friendly face and a bit of banter.

Her job was to make sure office workers weren't without a cuppa and a biscuit during the day, usually around mid-morning and mid-afternoon.

It wasn't all that long ago either. I'm sure we still had tea ladies at the radio station I worked at until the late '80s. It seems almost unbelievable in this day and age of corporate downsizing and budget cuts, but tea ladies were considered to be an important part of office structure, making sure that employees were looked after and their needs were catered for.

Tea ladies were eventually phased out and replaced with tea and coffee dispensers and a move to a more modern workplace where workers make, or more often than not, buy their own hot drinks and snacks during breaks. While the job has gone, executives in some offices still have an employee who takes care of their tea or coffee order as part of their other duties.

Can you still recall tea ladies in your workplace?

The good old days when you didn't have to go out and buy your own hot drink

Photo by News Ltd/Newspix

Something you don't see much of today

Flickr

Do kids still have to do the washing up after the evening meal like we used to?

I notice my grandchildren are not required to take turns at washing and drying the dishes after tea (or dinner) as everything just goes in the dishwasher. I was thinking about it and you know, while we hated having to do the dishes, looking back, there was a fair bit of family bonding going on during the exercise.

We would have squabbles about whose turn it was to wash or dry, this plate is not clean enough, you're drying too slow, etc., etc., but there would also be some good-natured banter too about all sorts of family things, what was going on at school and the like. Our parents probably picked up a fair bit of knowledge about what we were doing away from home just by listening in to the conversation.

Maybe we should ditch the dishwasher and get the kids back to the sink. What do you think?

On Guy Fawkes night the whole neighbourhood would come together to build a big bonfire with a 'Guy' on top

Courtesy of Jennifer Smart

Remember, remember 5 November?

Most Baby Boomers will remember it as Guy Fawkes or cracker night.

The story of Guy Fawkes is pretty well known. He and his co-conspirators tried to blow up the Houses of Parliament in London on 5 November 1605. Following the failure of the plot, a special Act of Parliament was passed creating a day of thanksgiving every year.

The celebration of the day was brought to Australia by our English ancestors and regardless of the fact that most of the country is dry and inflammable at that time of year, we always celebrated Guy Fawkes day right around the nation.

The date was later changed to the cooler times of the year, but it was eventually banned because of safety concerns.

Thinking back now, I can't believe how dangerous it must have been, and there were injuries, some very serious.

It's a wonderful childhood memory though.

There was great excitement when television first arrived in Australia.

It came in 1956, with Melbourne and Sydney getting the first channels in time for the 1956 Melbourne Olympics.

TV transmission commenced in Brisbane, Adelaide and Perth in 1959. The wait and build-up seemed to go on forever before it finally arrived.

Electrical retailers around the country attracted large crowds of people, eager to see television for the first time. Even local councils got involved by demonstrating trial telecasts.

It was not unusual for crowds to stand for hours just watching a test pattern and a few black and white flickering frames as Channel 9, Channel 7 and the ABC prepared to launch later in the year.

The first family in the street to get TV would usually invite neighbours and friends around for a night of TV viewing.

Crowds watching TV at an electrical retailer in the 1950s

Photo by News Ltd/Newspix

'The voice of cricket' at work in a booth at
Adelaide Oval in Adelaide, 1982

Photo by News Ltd/Newspix

'Maaaaarvellous'. Remember the 'voice of cricket' during the summer months? Considered one of the greatest all-rounders, up there with 'The Don', Richie Benaud was the first cricketer to achieve the Test double of 2000 runs and 200 wickets. A lethal leg spinner, in the late 1950s and early '60s, Benaud helped Australia dominate world cricket and went on to become Australia's Test captain in 1958. After retiring from the game in 1964, Benaud became one of the greatest commentators in world cricket. He had a wry understated sense of humour and a great selection of off-white jackets. After a long battle with skin cancer, Benaud died peacefully in his sleep in 2015.

#18

FACT

In 1973, Patrick White became the first Australian to win the Nobel Prize for Literature. Many Australians found his work a little frightening, but the Nobel reminded us that there was a thing called Australian Literature, and it was interesting, and it even won awards. Thank you, Patrick White.

Author Colleen McCulloch with her book *The Thorn Birds*, 1977. Was it 'the great Australian novel'?

Photo by Barry McKinnon/Newspix

Colleen McCulloch was a larger-than-life character and a prolific writer whose popular novel, *The Thorn Birds*, became a huge success and an international best seller in 1977.

Colleen's literary agent was a good friend of mine so I had the chance to meet her on a number of occasions, enjoy her company and talk to her about some of the influences in her life.

Although *The Thorn Birds* was her most successful work, she did not believe it was her best and indeed went on to write many fine novels.

For a while in the late '70s, I recall some critics hailing *The Thorn Birds* as 'the great Australian novel', likening it to *Gone With the Wind*, and its success continued, when in 1983, it was made into a television mini-series, which became the United States' second highest rated mini-series of all time behind 'Roots'.

Colleen died at her home on Norfolk Island in January 2015.

1974

1974 was the worst Christmas Darwin residents ever experienced. With wind gusts of up to 240 kilometres per hour lashing the city, 90 per cent of homes were destroyed or badly damaged. Residents were warned on Christmas Eve that Cyclone Tracy was expected to make landfall on Christmas morning, but this was ignored by most as Darwin had already experienced a near-miss from Cyclone Selma a few weeks earlier – people felt somewhat invincible. Tracy was classified as a Category 4, which is the second-highest level on the intensity scale. The Bureau of Meteorology describes a Category 4: 'Significant roofing loss and structural damage. Many caravans destroyed and blown away. Dangerous airborne debris. Widespread power failures.' Many experts believe Tracy was a Category 5 ('Extremely dangerous with widespread destruction') before landfall. On that terrible day in 1974, 65 innocent souls lost their lives and 145 people were admitted to hospital with serious injuries.

After the cyclone 30 000 Darwin residents were evacuated, many never returning

Photo by News Ltd/Newspix

Remember when Christmas school holidays rolled around? Seven weeks of complete freedom, and boy what freedom we enjoyed! Over the 'end of year' school holidays, our parents would rarely see us as we took off for adventures, down the beach, dive bombing off the end of the jetty, swimming in the creek or river, riding our bikes down to the dump to search for treasures, playing cricket out in the street and on a hot night, sleeping out on the front or back lawn.

Children of the '50s and the '60s were less supervised and had much more freedom than today's kids. Parents now are concerned with 'stranger danger' or whether their children may be experimenting with drugs or watching something harmful on the internet or might be involved in an accident riding their bikes. In the '50s those kind of dangers either did not exist or our parents completely ignored them.

I can't blame today's parents for their concerns, but growing up back then was far simpler and seemed a much more innocent time.

School holidays! Could things get any better?!

Photo by News Ltd/Newspix

Sunday morning after church, we all had our little jobs to do. Sunday was always family day at home, or sometimes a drive to nowhere in particular

Photo by News Ltd/Newspix

Sunday was a real family day. On a Sunday morning after church, we all had our chores to do.

Back then, almost everybody in our street went to church on a Sunday morning. Afterwards it would be back home to read the funny pages in the paper and do little odd jobs before the Sunday roast.

I can recall helping Dad with the gardening and raking up all the dog poo, while my sisters helped Mum with preparing the roast and making cakes and biscuits for the coming week.

My wife remembers her particular job for weekly pocket money was to clean all the hair brushes.

What are your memories of those Sunday family days?

Old wooden school desk – unusually no names,
or art carved into the wooden top!

Courtesy of Robert Mallin

What is your fondest memory of
schooldays?

I was a milk monitor and an ink monitor
and seeing these old desks, complete with
inkwell, takes me back to filling up the
inkwells from a bottle, a highly prized job
I might add, along with putting down the
school chairs in the morning.

We had those exact desks at school and
I remember the inkwells were collected
a couple of times a week, emptied and
re-filled. I also remember one of the girls
at school having one of her plaits dipped in
the inkwell by the boy who sat behind her.
From memory he got a six hander with the
cane.

#19
FACT

In February 1965 a group of
University of Sydney students,
including Charles Perkins,
took a bus tour of western
and coastal NSW towns. The
Freedom Ride, as it became
known, helped to highlight the
terrible discrimination faced by
Aboriginal people and sought
to improve relations between
Aboriginal people and white
Australians. The tour generated
huge media interest and
sparked a national debate about
the treatment of Aboriginal
Australians, a discussion that
resonated with voters in the
successful 1967 referendum for
Aboriginal rights.

Oh the horror! Australian Prime Minister William McMahon was upstaged by his wife Sonia at a White House State Dinner hosted by President Richard Nixon in November 1971. Sonia McMahon arrived wearing a split dress that was described at the time as being split to the thighs and armpits and held together by rhinestones! Upon seeing her President Nixon incredulously asked 'My God, who is that?' and insisted that she enter the dinner next to him. Never one to miss a media opportunity, Nixon knew that having Mrs McMahon by his side he'd be on the front pages of every US paper the following day.

'My God, who is that?'

Photo by News Ltd/Newspix

Australia was a conservative place during the '50s and early '60s, with social values to match. At the time, almost 90 per cent of the population identified as Christian. With perfect timing the American evangelist Billy Graham began his 15-week 'Southern Cross Crusade' in the late '50s. An astounding three million Australians attended his countrywide rallies as he travelled to Melbourne, Launceston, Hobart, Sydney, Brisbane, Canberra, Adelaide and Perth. Tens of thousands

of Australians converted, including Anglican Archbishop Peter Jensen, who recently commented 'without the Graham crusades, I think our churches would be in a far worse place than they are now.'

Around 70 000 people clamour to hear Billy Graham's message at the Sidney Myer Music Bowl in February 1959

Photo by News Ltd/Newspix

BOB BOLTS IN

Mal quits in tears

The Sun
NEWS-PICTORIAL

PHONE 63-0211 (Classified 63-0351) 25c

Melbourne, Monday, March 7, 1983

64 Pages — Including 4-Page Turf Guide

64 Pages

WEATHER — Bureau City forecast: Cool change. Showers. Expected top 27. Y'day 32.
● Details — Page 30.

601,826
Average daily sale

● TRIUMPH! Labor Party leader Bob Hawke raises the hand of his wife Hazel in salute on Saturday night as the poll count showed he'd won. Mr Hawke had just claimed victory in the national tally room in Canberra. Picture: ALEX GALL.

From PETER REES

CANBERRA — Australia's Prime Minister-elect, Mr Hawke, took the first steps to form a government yesterday after a sweeping victory in Saturday's elections.

The Labor Party won with a 4.9 per cent swing that took 21 seats from the Liberal-National Party Government.

The Prime Minister, Mr Fraser, admitted defeat in a dignified but emotional statement at Melbourne's Southern Cross Hotel just after 1 a.m. yesterday.

He shocked supporters and opponents alike by announcing he would quit as party leader immediately.

Seconds later he was in tears as his son Mark, manager of the family property Nareen, grabbed him in a bearhug.

Mr Hawke began taking over the reins of government yesterday.

He contacted the Treasury Secretary, Mr John Stone, and called for a report on the size of the Budget deficit amid reports that it could be higher than the $4 billion announced by the Government.

Speculation

Mr Hawke received the report later in the day and said he would probably release the document today.

The Treasurer-elect, Mr Keating, also had talks with Government officials and bankers to discuss the outflow of currency in the past few weeks which has led to speculation about a devaluation.

Late yesterday Mr Fraser called on the Governor-General, Sir Ninian Stephen, who asked him to stay on as caretaker Prime Minister until the Labor Ministry is sworn in on Friday.

In the Liberal leadership race, the Employment and Industrial Relations Minister, Mr Peacock, 44, and the Treasurer, Mr Howard, 43, are expected to nominate.

Sir Ninian yesterday commissioned Mr Hawke to form a government. Labor MPs will meet on Thursday to elect the ministry.

At the close of counting yesterday Labor had won 73 seats, the Liberals 29, the Nationals 18 with five doubtful.

HERE COME THE FIRST OF THE BOAT PEOPLE!

Poll results in full

The front page of *The Sun* shows a jubilant Bob Hawke with his then wife Hazel

Photo by News Ltd/Newspix

Union leader and Rhodes Scholar Bob Hawke, the 'Silver Bodgie', led Labor out of the political wilderness and became Prime Minister on 5 March 1983 after defeating the Liberals in a landslide. It was the greatest Labor victory in 40 years – when John Curtin won two-thirds of the seats in the House of Representatives. In 1983, Labor won 75 seats out of the 125. Hawke went on to lead the country for eight and half years, until successfully challenged by Paul Keating in the middle of 'the recession we had to have'.

#20
FACT

When Australian-born feminist Germaine Greer published her now famous book, *The Female Eunuch*, in 1970 it stirred a lot of controversy and debate. Written with a sense of humour and honesty, it was hugely successful and helped the reinvigorate the Women's Liberation Movement. *The Female Eunuch* is one of the most influential books ever written on women's roles in society.

Sue Becker shot to fame in Australia in the late '60s with a TV fitness segment which was called 'Swing in Time'. Followers on our Facebook website remember her for the black leotard she always wore, how incredibly nimble she was and how she drank a glass of champagne while demonstrating how to exercise!

She returned to the UK in the mid-70s where she recorded a series of half hour exercise workouts called 'Boomph with Becker', which were picked up and aired by the BBC.

Sue died from cancer in 2007.

Sue Becker – the Jane Fonda of her day

Photo by News Ltd/Newspix

At school we used to do 'French knitting' also called a 'tomboy' or a 'knitting nancy'

ARW

Remember making 'tomboys' at school?

In some parts of Australia it was called 'French knitting' and nowadays I believe its referred to as a 'knitting nancy'.

My grandmother used to hammer four tacks into the top of an old wooden cotton reel and then we'd weave a woollen thread around the four tacks and pull it through the hole in the reel. Why? I'm not sure what they were ever used for, but I do recall that every now and again there would be a bit of a craze on these at school and all the kids would be making a tomboy.

Come to think of it, they may have been those little woollen mats that lived under the teapot.

Apparently kids still do this sort of thing today, but don't have the wooden cotton reels.

These were pretty big in the '50s and '60s from memory.

Gold Coast Meter Maids were first introduced in 1965 to help beat the bad image created by the installation of parking meters along the famous tourist strip.

Having girls dressed in very scanty gold bikinis with gold tiaras, stroll up and down the tourist area and feed coins into any expired meters was very controversial.

When the Gold Coast was battered by storms in 1967, the then mayor, Sir Bruce Small, took the girls on a promotional tour around Australia to get people back to the beaches.

That idea proved so successful that it gained publicity not only in Australia but around the world and the meter maids became something of a Gold Coast institution.

People look on as as Gold Coast Meter Maid, Julie Hopgood, does her job

Photo by News Ltd/Newspix

1965

Lionel Rose made history in 1968 when he became the first Aboriginal Australian to be crowned a world champion boxer

Photo by News Ltd/Newspix

Lionel Rose was a national hero when he defeated Japanese world bantamweight champion, Fighting Harada, over 15 gruelling rounds in Tokyo in 1968.

His was a true 'Aussie battler' story, having started out the son of a boxer and gradually working his way from the bush to the city and eventually on to the international boxing circuit.

After his win in Tokyo, Lionel was given a public reception at the Melbourne Town Hall, which was witnessed by more than 100 000 people. His professional fighting career spanned 11 years from 1964 to 1975 with 42 wins (12 by a knockout) and 11 losses.

During the '70s Lionel also embarked on a singing career and managed a couple of very successful hit songs with 'I Thank You' and 'Please Remember Me'.

He died on 8 May 2011 after a short illness.

#21
FACT

Australia's first 'test tube baby' was born in 1980 amid controversy about the ethics of artificially manipulating human procreation in this way. We've moved a long way since then and it's estimated that nearly 13 000 IVF babies were born in Australia in 2012 alone. Today over 3 per cent of all babies born in Australia are IVF babies. Amazing to think of the number of Australians alive today because of this fantastic technology.

The Monkees toured Australia in 1968 attracting huge crowds of screaming fans not seen since the Beatles toured in 1964

Photo by Barry O'Brien/Newspix

'Hey , Hey, We're the Monkees'... Remember when the Monkees came to Australia in 1968?

The group's American members were Micky Dolenz, Michael Nesmith, Peter Tork, and Englishman Davy Jones. They began their tour of Australia in September 1968. By that time, they had achieved worldwide success with a string of chart-topping singles and a television comedy series, which from memory was on TV every afternoon. Thousands of fans turned out to welcome them and after performing in Melbourne and Sydney the group travelled on to Brisbane, arriving on Sunday, 22 September. Over 3000 screaming fans were at the Brisbane Airport to greet them from behind a safety fence with police keeping a close watch. *The Courier Mail* reported that 'a cavalcade of five cars carried the entertainers and their party from their plane past the yelling, waving crowd'.

Did you get to the concert?

A young Graham Kennedy enjoys a cup of tea with radio greats, including Bob Dyer and Jack Davey

Photo by News Ltd/Newspix

When the wireless was king, the radio personalities who ruled the airwaves were treated like movie stars, commanded big salaries, and were adored by their fans. However, radio changed forever in the late '50s with the introduction of TV and many of the stars from that era quickly moved onto the small screen. The mainstays of the old wireless, including quiz shows, comedy programs and radio serials, suddenly had less appeal to listeners who could watch similar shows on TV. At first it looked like the new medium would be the death of the old, but radio found two new niches where it was able to compete, news, and eventually talkback.

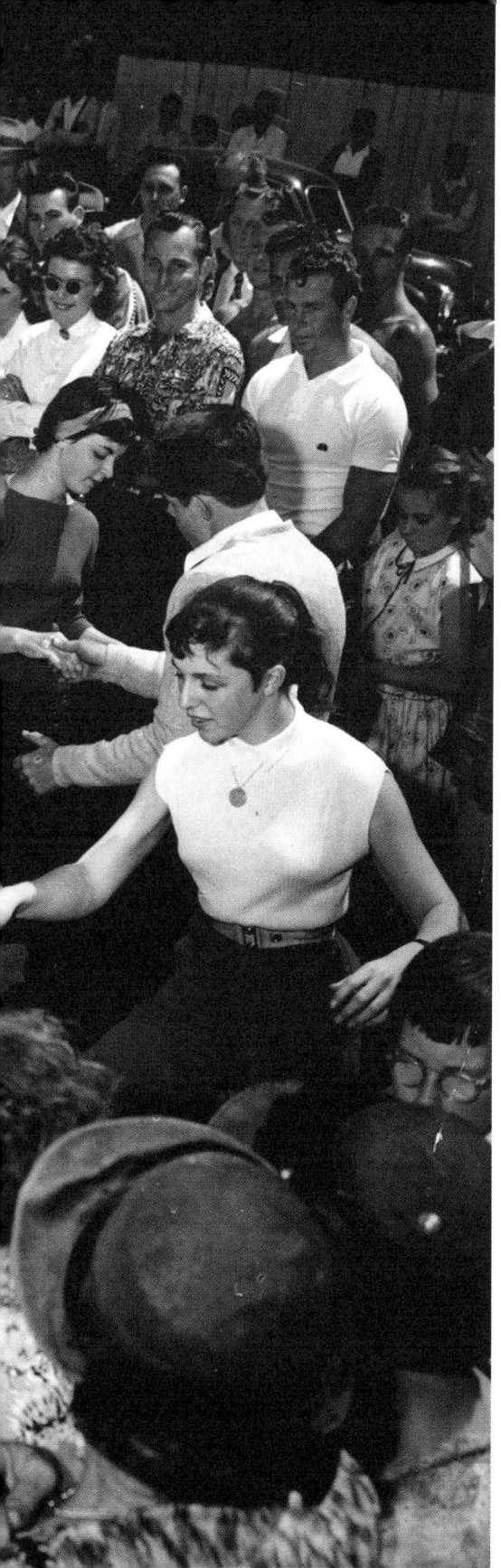

Can you remember learning the jive?

Jiving was associated with rock 'n' roll music, which first appeared in the mid-50s and was widely condemned by church groups and authorities as evil and the 'work of the devil'. The best jivers were called bodgies and widgies – they wore stovepipe pants and sloppy joes, and were initially considered to be trouble-makers and even juvenile delinquents.

Many young people in those days were branded rebels simply because they loved the new music and the dancing that went with it. Many of my friends, who did not drink alcohol, smoke and were still virgins, were labelled 'bad' because of the way they dressed and had their hair cut.

Teenagers in the early 1960s doing the jive

Photo by News Ltd/Newspix

Many people have strong memories of arriving in Australia as the child of a migrant family. For most of those families their first 'home' was a Nissan Hut at one of the many migrant hostels dotted around the suburbs and some country areas of Australia from the '40s to the '70s.

Life was pretty tough, not just for the parents, but for the kids who were sent straight to school, many not being able to speak any English. Life was a lot tougher for both old and new Australians back then, without the modern conveniences, luxuries and money that many modern day Australians consider their birth right.

I often wonder how Gen X or Gen Y would react if they were asked to live in a non air-conditioned hut without mod cons, in a barren, stark environment for several years while waiting for a house and a job.

Immigrant husband and wife team, William (known as Bill) and Esmeralda (known as Ral) at work inside the grocer's shop

Migration Museum collection PN05822, courtesy of Mrs J Moore

The Grocery Store at Gepps Cross Hostel in Adelaide, painted with advertising

Migration Museum collection PN05822, courtesy of Mrs J Moore

In the 1970s, the green phone was found in almost every suburb in Australia. It was solid metal and was the target of many a coin thief

Courtesy of Henry Titchen

Who remembers the old public telephones?

Long before there were mobile phones, iPads, computers or even Facebook, if you were out and about and wanted to get in touch with your family or friends, you had to find a public phone, and one that worked too – many of them didn't work because they'd been vandalised. You'd have to feed the money into the slot, and if it was an interstate call you'd better have a few dollars in coins sitting on the top of the phone waiting too.

Australia Remember When poster Kim Bell remembers when she lived in Queensland and didn't have a home phone: 'I'd have to drive to the phone booth with a pocket full of coins to ring my sister in Adelaide to catch up.'

How on earth did we all survive without mobile phones?

#22
FACT

Have you planted an Arbor Day tree? Arbor Day has been observed in Australia since 1889. A hundred years later Prime Minister Bob Hawke pledged to plant one billion trees as Australia grappled with land degradation. Seven-hundred million trees were planted before the government lost the 1996 election and the program was scrapped. Planet Ark's National Tree Day and Schools Tree Day replaced it. Since 1996, three million people have planted 21 million trees.

Bob Dyer (*left*) and Jack Davey were the absolute superstars of the wireless in the '50s

Photo from News Ltd/Newspix

Remember the days when the wireless was the main form of evening entertainment? We'd all gather around and watch the radio and listen to programs like 'The Ampol Show' with Jack Davey or 'Pick-a-Box' with Bob Dyer.

Davey and Dyer were the undisputed kings of the airwaves back then, genuine superstars of the era.

Davey was a wonderfully talented showman who started out as the breakfast announcer on 2GB Sydney in the mid-30s. By 1955 he was compere of at least half a dozen nationally broadcast radio shows, including the 'Ampol Show', 'Give It a Go' among other programs. In 1957 he added TV to his outstanding resume, with three regular national programs for Channel 7, but his health began to suffer.

Davey died in October 1959 and a reported crowd of 150 000 people attended his funeral at St Andrew's Anglican Cathedral in Sydney.

Dyer was American by birth and came to Australia in 1937, playing the ukulele as part of a hillbilly show. He established himself on radio during the 1940s and '50s compering quiz programs that often included elaborate gags and stunts.

His well-known catch-cries were 'The money or the box?', 'Happy lathering customers' and 'Tell them Bob sent you'. His shows included, 'Winner Take All', 'Cop the Lot' and 'Pick-a-Box', which he later took on to national TV.

Bob died in January 1984.

Long before the days of cling film!

ARW

Who can remember when you used to take your lunch to school wrapped in grease-proof or wax paper and placed inside a brown paper bag?

Fritz or devon and tomato sauce sandwiches, Vegemite, Camp Pie with sauce or maybe some silverside.

I don't recall having a lunch box as such, and my school bag always had that slightly stale-food smell. I can almost smell it now just thinking about it!

I remember too that we had to bring the sandwich paper and paper bag home so that it could be used again next day, and the next and the next.

Whatever happened to frugal living?

By the mid-1960s thousands of girls around Australia would proudly don their uniform and boots and march every week in a marching girls team.

The *Australian Women's Weekly* published an article about the marching girls teams in June 1966: 'They march through the streets, at parks, in playing fields. They march at football matches, carnivals and fetes. A festive occasion in Australia isn't complete without a team of marching girls these days.'

The sport survives and is known today as Drill Dance.

Balwyn Returned and Service's League Grenadels Marching Girls Team, 1969, with medals on bandoliers around their necks

Museum Victoria. Reg. No: MM 110399

'Molly' Meldrum was instrumental in establishing Australia's first pop music newspaper *Go Set* and was compere of 'Countdown' on ABC TV

Photo by Noel Kessel/Newspix

It seems like Molly Meldrum has been around the Australian pop music scene since it first began. In fact, he started out with *Go Set* newspaper back in 1966, writing a weekly gossip column for the paper, which led on to regular feature stories. He went on to become a highly respected reviewer of newly released records.

Go Set folded in 1974 and about the same time, ABC TV was looking for somebody to regularly front a segment for its new pop music show, 'Countdown'. Molly got the gig and, it worked so well and he became so popular, he ended up being the compere of the entire program by the end of the year.

The final episode of Countdown was shown in July 1987.

Molly went on to appear as guest on numerous other TV programs, write weekly columns for various newspapers and even produced a number of pop songs.

He remains one of Australia's favourite music personalities.

145

I started my working life at the age of 14 as a telegram boy in the Postmaster-General's Department.

Yes, I was at the cutting edge of communication technology in the late 1950s, with my red PMG bike and a telegram pouch, and if you wanted to get a message to somebody by the quickest means possible, I was probably your best bet.

It's almost funny now, looking back, but not everyone had the phone on and at that time, most people communicated by letter.

I often think it would be fascinating to be transported back to mid-last century again, just to experience how dawdling and leisurely life must have been.

It would be interesting, but I doubt that I'd want to stay!

Trainee telegram boys at GPO in Brisbane, 1950

Photo by Al Pascoe/Newspix

Remember the days when we had paper money in Australia?

Back in the '60s and '70s there were apparently lots of fraud $10 and $20 bank notes found to be in circulation. Fraudsters were simply using colour copying machines to come up with reasonably good facsimilies of our paper money and the Reserve Bank of the day decided to do something about it. Working with the CSIRO and the University of Melbourne they developed polymer, or

1988

Our colourful paper money before plastic notes

Courtesy of Daniel Winkless

plastic bank notess, which were extremely difficult to reproduce and included a number of other security features.

The first polymer bank notes were introduced in 1988 and by 1996 Australia was the first country in the world to switch completely to the new plastic money. Since then, many other nations around the world have invested in this technology and also gone to the plastic currency.

Wish I'd kept some of the old paper notes, purely for sentimental reasons!

There was a time when, as a child, flying on a plane with Mum and Dad, the air hostess would come down the aisle and invite you to go up to the cockpit and watch the pilots fly.

It was a fantastic experience for any child, but even as I'm writing this I'm thinking, 'Wow! The parents let the child out of their sight for 10 minutes, allowing them to be taken, completely unchaperoned, into a cabin of complete strangers.'

How times have changed! These days the cockpit is off limits to everyone, even children. I realise that one needs to move with the times, but sometimes moving with the times doesn't necessarily make things better.

Hindmarsh School students skipping during PE class, 1954

Photo by News Ltd/Newspix

When you flew with your parents you were made a member and received a little badge with wings

ARW

Physical education was a regular part of school from the '50s, and it was pretty gruelling too as far as I remember. Students were required to do pull-ups, push-ups and sit-ups, skipping, running, marching, obstacle courses and more.

We spent a lot of our waking hours outdoors anyway, riding the bike to and from school, and at recess and during lunch hour nobody was allowed to stay indoors – we would run all over the schoolyard playing physical games.

There weren't many obese kids back then and although I never really enjoyed competitive sport, I had to get involved and take part.

Who watched 'The Sullivans' on TV in the late '70s to early '80s?

We would tune in every week to see what was happening in the lives of this all-Australian family and their neighbours, relatives and acquaintances. The Sullivans ended up being shown in many countries all over the world.

The story began in 1939, when war was declared against Germany. The majority of the show's storylines related to the war, the fighting and the effects of the war on the family.

There was the Dad, Dave Sullivan, and his wife, Grace, and the kids, John, Tom, Terry and Kitty.

Many followers of the show couldn't believe it when Grace was killed off while she was in England, but the program continued on successfully until 1982, when the war ended in the storyline and the series came to an end.

The cast of 'The Sullivans', 1976

Photo by News Ltd/Newspix

An original Commonwealth Bank Money Box

Courtesy of Antique Effects, Ballarat

#23
FACT

What do cocoa, copha, desiccated coconut, icing sugar and Rice Bubbles make? There's only one answer: Chocolate Crackles. First printed on a Kellogg's cereal box in 1953, this treat has been enjoyed at children's parties for decades since then. And you don't even need to cook them!

There was a time when pocket money was something that had to be earned and never given freely.

I was reminded of how tough it was to get pocket-money out of my parents when my wife reminded me that one of her pocket-money jobs was to regularly wash and clean the hairbrushes at home.

I remember my job of a Sunday morning was to rake up all the dog's droppings and to push the hand mower over the front lawn. My sisters had to help prepare the Sunday roast and also help Mum bake biscuits and a cake while the wood stove was fired up (later the electric stove). Most parents in the '50s and '60s were very frugal and after all the household bills were paid from the single-income pay packet, I imagine there would not have been a lot left.

I know that some kids today still have to do chores to get their pocket money, but for us it was never guaranteed.

The trade counter at Harris Scarfe store in Adelaide, 1960

Photo by News Ltd/Newspix

Whatever happened to the personal customer service and home deliveries that were provided by grocers, greengrocers and other local shops and businesses in the '50s and '60s? Most of it came to an end of course with the spread of the big supermarkets and shopping centres around Australia from the mid-1960s. Self-service with products stacked on shelves, shopping trolleys and check out chicks meant the end of an era when the customer was served on a one-on-one personal level. The arrival of the big suburban shopping centres also brought to an end the weekly shopping trip to 'town' once a week by Mum to replenish the kitchen cupboard.

There are still some smaller businesses, and a few large companies, that offer good

Olivia Newton John and 'Molly' Meldrum on the set of 'Countdown' in the early '80s

Photo by News Ltd/Newspix

service but they are few and far between, and to be honest we, the customers, have brought a lot of this on ourselves. In an effort to keep our own cost of living down we chase the cheaper products and brands, which of course generally come from a business with lower overheads, fewer staff and very little or no service. It's a vicious circle, we still want that wonderful customer service we had back in the '50s and '60s, but we don't really want to pay extra.

Born in England and raised in Melbourne, Olivia Newton-John became a household name after she played terribly well-behaved and squeaky clean Sandy in the movie *Greece*, which was one of the most successful musicals in movie history. Her next movie, *Xanadu*, had much less success, but undeterred Newton-John went on to hit the charts with her song, 'Magic'. She followed this up with her hugely successful hit single, 'Let's Get Physical', where she went for a sexy, athletic look that no doubt helped sales! Newton-John's life became quieter when she started a family in 1986. After surviving a breast-cancer diagnosis in the early '90s, Newton-John went on to produce a line of wellness products for women.

Evonne Goolagong became a household name around Australia in the '70s and early '80s. She was a fantastic tennis player and a great ambassador for the nation, winning 14 Grand Slam titles, including the Australian Open, Wimbledon and the French Open. She was awarded Australian of the Year in 1971 and was appointed an MBE in 1972. By the mid-70s she was at the peak of her career and married Roger Cawley. Less than 12 months later she was ranked number one in the world.

Evonne and Roger had a daughter in 1977 before she went on to win Wimbledon again in 1980, making her the only mother to have won the coveted title, since World War I.

In 1985, Evonne Goolagong Cawley was inducted into the Sport Australia Hall of Fame and in 1988 into the International Tennis Hall of Fame.

She currently lives with her husband and two children at Noosa Heads in Queensland.

Evonne Goolagong holding the winner's trophy at the 1971 Dutch Open

Wikipedia

A Kodak 'Instamatic' camera. These days everyone has a camera in their pocket

dreamstime

Did you own a Kodak 'Instamatic' back in the '60s?

The first Instamatics went on sale in early 1963 and had an easy-load film cartridge and a little pop-up flash, later replaced with flashbulb cubes. A wide variety of print and slide film was sold by Kodak for the instamatic range.

They were said to be in the tradition of Kodak's earlier Brownie cameras, providing a simple snapshot camera anyone could use.

I've never really been into photography, but even I had one of these back in the day.

Everybody has an instant camera in their pocket these days with their mobile phones. Nowadays people can take a photo at the drop of a hat – back then it was much more of an involved production!

Looking at the way kids are protected these days, how on earth did we ever survive in the '50s and '60s?

No car seats, no seat belts, no rubber matting or soft wood chips in the playground, no side nets on trampolines. We were allowed to climb trees, ride our bikes all over town, swim in the creeks, play football and cricket out in the street, play 'king of the castle' on piles of gravel left on construction sites. And if we got hurt Mum would pull out the bottle of iodine and we got our hair ruffled and were told to get back out there again. Now it's a trip to the emergency room and a 10-day dose of antibiotics.

One of my fondest memories was riding to the local dump (they were all open in those days) and searching for old wheels which we would attach to a billy cart. The cart would be made of an old apple crate nailed to a plank with a rope to turn the front wheels – and no brakes and no crash helmets! Skinned knees, elbows and gravel rash galore but when you went over, you got up, pushed the cart back to the top of the hill and did it all over again.

Andrew Heslop, Social Entrepreneur, Commentator and Community Advocate shared a photo and memories of the children's TV program, 'Romper Room':

Who remembers Channel 0/10's Romper Room? I was a regular performer on the show because the producers found it so hard to source outgoing kids not scared of the lights and cameras in the studio. Putting me on the show was my late mother's idea and it proved to be a very good introduction to my first job in radio where I worked with Bob Byrne.

I was such a 'helpful' child and understood the script that at the end of the show I would run to Miss Michele's desk and pass to her the Magic Mirror ... which was in two pieces, lilac and covered in silver glitter ... and then she would say hello to the girls and boys she could see at home.

Romper Room was a television franchise from America and stations bought the format to make locally.

You could write to the TV station and they would mail out a cardboard car (which was a box), to enable you to play along at home.

Billycarts were mostly constructed from bits we found at the local dump. A set of pram wheels, a plank, piece of rope and the steepest hill we could find!

Museum Victoria. Reg. No: MM 110102

Channel 0/10 would mail out the car for the kids to 'drive' while watching Romper Room

Courtesy of Andrew Heslop

Something to take you back to your childhood.
My wife would get one of these every year she
went to the Royal Show

Courtesy of the Original Kewpie Co
(www.theoriginalkewpieco.com)

It was a tradition in my wife's family that whenever they got to go to the Royal Show, she would get a kewpie doll on a stick. Still has one, although she's looking a little worse for wear after 50 years (the doll that is).

This photo created an amazing amount of interest when I posted it on the Australia Remember When Facebook website earlier this year, with many thousands of people commenting on the wonderful memories it brought back. Countless posters remembered collecting one every year, while others recalled that they always wanted one but somehow missed out.

Show bags were more my thing, but of course once I ate or played with all the contents, they disappeared into the dust of time.

#24
FACT

After Honolulu in Hawaii, Perth is the world's most isolated capital city. It is closer to Indonesia's capital city, Jakarta (3007 km), than to its own capital city of Canberra (3905 km by road). Sydney is over 4400 km away by road. Perth is also the most isolated city in Australia.

The iPod 1960s style!

dreamstime

Think the iPhone was a genius invention? Nothing compared to the transistor radio, which came onto the market in the mid to late '50s. What a wonderful invention. For the first time music was completely portable and we could listen to our favourite AM radio shows on the tranny.

I remember the first time I saw one of these 'tiny' radios was when I first started work in the PMG Department and a co-worker friend of mine bought his first transistor so he could listen to the cricket while delivering telegrams.

They were fairly expensive back then but I had to have one, so I purchased my first transistor with a Custom Credit Time Payment Plan.

Now I'm starting to feel ancient! Lol!

We didn't get a lot of toys, so we would make up games with whatever was available. Old jam tins were ideal to make tin-can telephones

ARW

What are some of the games you remember from childhood?

I posed this question to some Baby Boomer friends of mine and one game I hadn't recalled for a long time was making a telephone from a couple of tin cans. Remember that?

We used to punch a hole in the bottom of two old jam tins and connect them together with a length of string, then get as far away as the string would allow and magically, we could have a conversation through our tin-can telephone.

We didn't need digital devices then to keep ourselves entertained, just a couple of jam tins, a piece of string and heaps of imagination.

As kids we made do with what was available. Games would be simple like 'brandy', where all you needed was a single tennis ball and all the kids in the neighbourhood could join in and play. There was hopscotch, all you needed there was a piece of chalk, or 'red rover all over', nothing needed, just a group of kids.

We used to play cricket out on the road with an old bat and an apple crate as the wicket. The game would go on until it got dark and Mum would be yelling out for us to come and have tea (it wasn't called dinner in those days).

No fancy toys back then. How on earth did we manage to have a happy childhood?!

Tania Verstak was Miss Australia in 1961, and
went on to be crowned Miss International in 1962

Photo by News Ltd/Newspix

She was the most photographed woman
in Australia in 1962, and even today most
people from that era remember the name
Tania Verstak.

The most famous of all the Miss
Australias, Tania was born in 1942 in
Tianjin, China and came to Australia at
the age of seven with her Russian parents.
She spent her childhood in Manly and
by the age of 16 had blossomed into a
stunning beauty. She eventually won five
beauty quests from Miss Movie Ball and
Miss Sydney University, to Miss New
South Wales, Miss Australia in 1961 and
Miss International in 1962.

The story of the refugee child who
became one of the most recognised faces
in Australia had a fitting climax when she
married and retired from public life to
begin her family.

The wood fire was lit at about 5pm and the kitchen was always the warmest, most welcoming room in the house

Courtesy of 'Every Dish Tells a Story'

In winter, the kitchen was always the warmest place in the house because the fire would have been lit at about 5pm or so in preparation to cook tea (now called dinner).

I remember we all sat down at the kitchen table at about 6.30 to eat and we'd listen to the radio serials, including 'Yes What?' at 6.30 and 'Tarzan' at 6.45 while eating Mum's meat and three veg.

The kitchen stayed warm for the evening as we kids did our homework. Mum would mend socks and Dad would read the paper. If it was really cold we might light the kerosene heater for extra warmth. Many houses had open fireplaces and some older houses had fireplaces in the bedrooms.

In winter we all wore flannelette pyjamas and all the beds had flannelette sheets, top and bottom. We never had air conditioning back then, but we were never cold either!

What are your memories of how you kept warm before reverse cycle air conditioning?

The Sydney Harbour Bridge, along with the Opera House and the harbour, has become an iconic image of Australia the world over. No matter how many times I fly into Sydney that image never fails to take my breath away.

The bridge and the landscape around it have changed dramatically over the years as can be seen from this image, taken in 1961.

Sydney Harbour Bridge, 1961

Photo by Weston Langford

TV arrived in Australia in 1956 with the first black and white images broadcast by Channel 9 in Sydney

Courtesy of Channel Nine

How exciting it was when television first arrived in Australia!

The first broadcast was in Sydney on 16 September 1956, when Bruce Gyngell introduced the new medium with the words 'Good evening and welcome to television'.

The 1956 Melbourne Olympic Games was broadcast as a test transmission by all three television stations operating in Melbourne at the time.

Television was introduced to Queensland, South Australia and Western Australia in 1959, Tasmania the following year, and the Australian Capital Territory in 1962. Television was introduced to the Northern Territory in 1971.

For a while people would take their chairs, blankets and a thermos of tea and settle down in front of the local electrical retailer to watch TV. Then the first house in the street to get a set would have a TV night and invite all the neighbours round.

I still have memories of sitting in a darkened lounge room in a neighbour's house singing along with 'Mitch Miller and the Gang', an early TV program.

#25
FACT

Despite being perfect for Australia's hot weather and beach-going culture we can't lay claim to being the birthplace of the humble thongs. That honour goes to Egypt, where thongs first made an appearance around 4000BC! Worn throughout history since that time, Australia's love affair with thongs really took off when Dunlop released their 'Thongs' in 1959. Most thongs bought in Australia today are Havaianas – a Brazilian brand that produces over 150 million pairs a year!

It wasn't a Saturday night if you missed 'Hey Hey It's Saturday' with Daryl, Ossie and the gang

Courtesy of Channel Nine

Remember when we would religiously tune in every Saturday night to watch 'Hey Hey It's Saturday' on Channel 9?

The show ran for 27 years, starting back in 1971 as a morning cartoon show (from memory), and the last episode was shown on 20 November 1999. Its host throughout its entire run was Daryl Somers with his sidekick Ossie Ostrich.

Other important characters on the show included voiceover man, John Blackman (who was also Dickie Knee), Red Symons, Wilbur Wilde, Molly Meldrum and Russell Gilbert.

I particularly loved the talent segment 'Red Faces', but there was so much fun in the free wheeling show that you had the distinct impression that nobody knew what was going to happen next.

Whatever happened to those fun days of live TV?

Australia's own Woodstock, with peace, love and rock 'n' roll was first held on Australia Day in 1972 at Sunbury in Victoria.

The Sunbury Pop Festival has been accorded a legendary status in the history of Australian rock. It was held annually on a 620-acre private farm between Sunbury and Diggers Rest until 1975, with crowds of up to 45 000 people attending.

Did you go? Or perhaps more importantly, do you remember anything about it?!

166

Some of the fans that attended the Sunbury Pop Festival, 29 January 1974 – the UK band, Queen, played for the first time in Australia at Sunbury that year

Fairfax Syndication

1973

One of the great iconic buildings of the 20th century, and one of the biggest tourist attractions in Australia today

Flickr

'It is one of the great iconic buildings of the 20th century, an image of great beauty that has become known throughout the world – a symbol for not only a city, but a whole country and continent.'

So read the citation on the 'Pritzker Prize', architecture's highest honour, when it was awarded to Danish architect Jørn Utzon in 2003 for his design of the Sydney Opera House.

The grand building's story began in 1955 when the then Premier of New South Wales, Joseph Cahill, launched an international competition for the design of a new performing arts centre to be built on Bennelong Point. Utzon was announced the winner in 1957 – out of over 230 entries by architects from 32 countries. The prize was £5000.

The Sydney Opera House was completed in 1973 at a cost $102 million and was formally opened, amid great fanfare, by Queen Elizabeth II on 20 October 1973.

It is now one of the most popular tourist attractions in Australia with more than seven million visitors each year. Over 300 000 people participate annually in guided tours.

Queen Elizabeth II arrives by car for the opening of the Sydney Opera House, 1973

Photo by News Ltd/Newspix

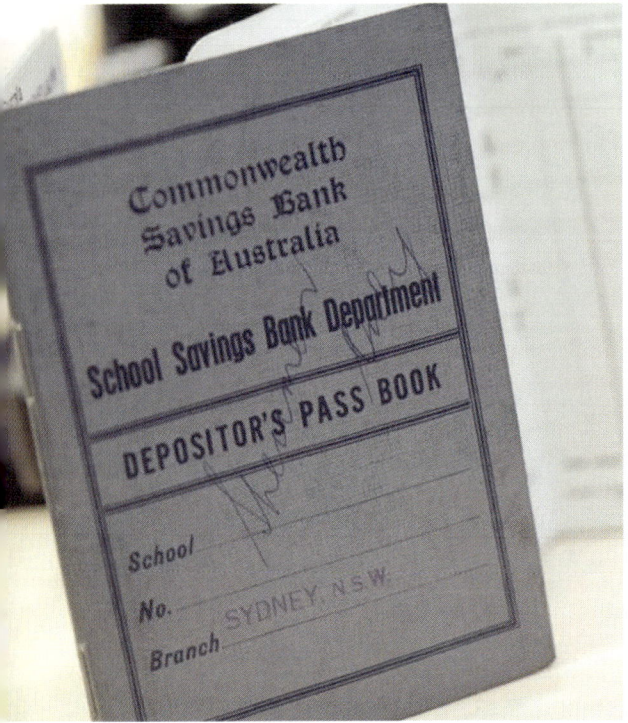

Mondays meant lining up to put 6d into my school bank account. Our parents taught us to be thrifty

Museum Victoria. Reg. No: HT 13699

I recall that Mondays were 'bank' days at school and we would take our bank books and 6d (I went to primary school in the '50s) and our school money of 2/-. I could never really see any point in saving money, when I could have put that 6d to good use, buying lollies or chewies!

I remember the cover of my Commonwealth Bank of Australia Bank Book being a dark grey in colour, with pages inside having figures written in the columns and little stamped entries.

Memories from long ago!

#26
FACT

Developed by Frank McEncroe, a boilermaker from Bendigo, in the early '50s, the Chiko Roll has become an Australian cultural icon! Made from cabbage, barley, carrot, beef tallow, cereal, celery and onion, the Chiko Roll made its first appearance at the Wagga Wagga Agriculture Show in 1951. At its peak 40 million Chiko Rolls were being sold annually in Australia. Since the advent of modern Australian cuisine the Chiko Roll doesn't sell so well, but it's still hugely popular.

On wet days we'd spend hours playing the board game 'Test Match'. When the sun was out, so were we, playing the real thing

Courtesy of Kerri Schrauf

I was thinking back to the days of the old 'Test Match' board game we used to play back in the '60s and '70s.

There are all sorts of new 'wizz-bang' cricket games around nowadays, especially some of the new digital games. I remember the two-dimensional edition where you had a number of players on the field – and if my memory serves me correctly – you pulled on a couple of cardboard tabs to randomly generate a type of delivery before your batting opponent did the same on the other end of the board and got a number of runs.

Mind you, if you were a genuinely competitive player, the reliance on luck would eventually start to grate and it became annoying when it was just pure good or bad luck that had you win or lose. The big advantage was that you could play it by yourself if you'd been banished to your bedroom.

Do you remember the old Test Match board game we used to play?

There used to be an old saying that Australians would bet on two flies crawling up the wall. But when it came to the question of allowing the construction of our first legal casino at Wrest Point, Hobart in 1968, the locals were almost evenly divided.

Some believed the Apple Isle should not cater to undesirables and heavy gamblers, while others thought a casino would benefit Tasmania's tourism and open up the area to the rest of the world.

A state referendum was held in December 1968 in which a narrow majority of Tasmanians voted in favour of the development. The Wrest Point Hotel Casino opened for business on 10 February 1973.

It's difficult to imagine now but back then, if you wanted to go to a casino, you had to travel to Macau or Las Vegas. Wrest Point changed all that and it wasn't long before every state had its own casino.

Wrest Point Casino opened in 1973. Until then Australia did not have any casinos at all

Wikipedia

'Ask the Leyland Brothers' was great family TV viewing from the 1970s

Photo by News Ltd/Newspix

'Ask the Leyland Brothers' ran from about 1976 to 1980, and again from 1983 to 1984 and provided most Australian viewers with their first look at outback Australia.

I seem to recall it was on Saturday or Sunday evening at around 5.30pm. It was a great show for the family, and of course educational for adults as well as kids.

The format of the show was driven by people writing in to Mike and Mal and asking a question about a part of Australia, which the brothers would then drive to and answer the question.

They did all their own filming and took their wives and children with them on most occasions. It was like watching a home movie and would probably never work on TV today, but back in the '70s it was a huge hit with audiences of several million watching every weekend.

Mike Leyland, sadly died a few years ago.

A container of dripping. I used to love bread and dripping, and back in the day most of our food was cooked in dripping or fat

Wikipedia

#27
FACT

'Shaddup You Face' by Joe Dolce topped the charts in Australia in 1980. A huge hit around the world, it holds the record for most successful Australian-produced music single ever: seems unlikely for a comic song about an Italian boy having a fight with his mother. But few would know that Dolce himself is now a theatre and cabaret artist, and an acclaimed poet.

Remember when Grandma would give you bread and dripping as a treat?

Before low-fat cooking oils were even thought of, most people cooked with dripping. The dripping was the congealed animal fat and blood from a previously cooked meal, with a strong salty flavour. Generous dollops of dripping were used to bake potatoes and other vegies, and also used to add extra flavour to meat. I recall that when my grandmother cooked with dripping the meals would have a much saltier flavour. She lived to be 90 and I imagine had always cooked in dripping. On occasion, she would give us bread and dripping, and although it was originally a way to punish children for not eating their meals, my sisters and I loved Grandma's treat.

Don't think I could eat it now though!! Did you eat bread and dripping as a child?

'It's as noisy as a Coles Cafeteria' became an Australian saying back in the '50s and '60s – and was used to describe a very noisy place

Courtesy of Coles

Long before fast-food chains arrived in Australia, the main emporiums and department stores had a cafeteria-style dining room, offering the 'fast food' of the day.

Ahhh! The memories! To a kid, on a rare shopping 'trip to town' with Mum and Grandma, it was heaven on a stick to be able to choose mains, desert, a drink and not to eat something home-made for a change.

To a young child, Coles Cafeteria was a wondrous place. It always seemed so large, so many tables and so crowded. There was a plastic tray that you pushed along the shelf and in front of you the 'bain marie' full of steaming hot food, served by the matronly ladies in their white coats, always offering a large dollop of gravy. I loved my banana splits or mixed sundaes, but I always felt more grown up if I selected the trifle because I knew it contained a little bit of sherry.

Remember the 'The Mike Walsh Show'? It was an Australian institution, which ran from 1973 to 1984 and was on air for 90 minutes every weekday afternoon.

The show was syndicated to regional television stations around Australia. Richard Neville, Jeanne Little and John-Michael Howson were frequent guests.

The program won a total of 24 Logie awards over the years, including a Gold Logie for Jeanne Little in 1977, and again for the host, Mike Walsh, in 1980. That same year saw the show awarded the Media Peace Prize by the United Nations. Walsh himself was appointed an Officer of the Order of the British Empire or the OBE.

I believe Mike now lives in London where he is still involved in theatre and television production.

Mike Walsh, Ita Buttrose and Mike 'Shirley' Williams at Mike Walsh's 21 Years in TV party, Sydney, 1981

Photo by News Ltd/Newspix

Before suburban swimming pools, kids used to keep cool in one of these

Museum Victoria. Reg. No. MM 110513

On a hot Australian summer's day, before the average household could afford air conditioning, we always found a way to keep cool – whether it was off to the beach on our bikes, playing under the sprinkler on the back lawn or improvising with one of these little aboveground canvas kids' pools.

I believe these first appeared in the early '70s. I can remember staying up until all hours one very hot Christmas Eve trying to assemble one of these so that Father Christmas could deliver it under the tree the following morning. Just seeing this photo now brings back so many memories of my children, happily playing for hours and keeping cool in their little wading pool.

Did you or your kids have one of these too?

We always used to get lolly or sugar eggs at Easter – they were beautifully decorated and delicious

Courtesy of Pittsworth Confectionary

Whatever happened to lolly or sugar Easter eggs?

All the eggs seem to be chocolate nowadays. I can remember as a kid we hardly ever got chocolate eggs, but every Easter the Easter Bunny would leave us a couple of these lolly Easter eggs.

I reckon they came as rabbits too and I seem to recall a chook-shaped lolly egg. They were joined around the middle with squiggly icing, which you always ate first – and there were little lollies inside too.

Can you remember these lolly Easter eggs? I haven't seen them in years.

Remember collecting old bottles for the Boy Scout's 'Bob's for Jobs'?

Photo by News Ltd/Newspix

Bob's for Jobs was an annual fundraiser for the Boy Scouts. We all had to put on our scout's uniform and go knocking on doors, offering to do chores for a shilling, which was then handed in to the scout master. I think we might have got a badge to sew on the uniform if we made a certain amount.

I remember my mate Jimmy Smoker and me putting on our scout uniforms and going around knocking on doors asking for donations of empty cool drink bottles (worth 6d) or beer bottles (worth 3d a dozen). We would walk for miles around the neighbourhood, unsupervised by any adults, stacking up our billycarts full of bottles before dropping them off back at the Scout Hall. Kids today unfortunately will never know that freedom!

It was in the '50s and '60s that Australia's food-shopping habits began to change.

Until then the weekly shop was mainly carried out at smaller, privately owned grocery shops and greengrocers, but in 1952 the first of the 'self-service' grocery stores began to appear. They were an immediate success and were still usually run by the store owners who continued to offer personal customer service.

G J Coles started to see that the real future was in supermarkets, and in 1957 followed Woolworths into food retailing, creating chains of supermarkets across the nation. It was in 1958 when one Sydney newspaper reported the 'battle of the self-service food stores may now be really on.'

Both Coles and Woolworths expanded rapidly, closely following the American model until they dominated food retailing in Australia.

By the early 1960s shopping habits had changed from small grocery shops to the larger self-service stores

Photo by News Ltd/Newspix

Remember Mr Movies?

Bill Collins was a schoolteacher in Sydney who started out writing movie reviews in the early 1960s, which landed him a gig as a film presenter at the ABC. He moved from the ABC to the Channel 9 working there between 1967 and 1974; moving again to Channel 7 and working there from 1975 to 1979. In 1980 he moved to Network Ten to present movies nationally. He is currently presenting movies on the Foxtel movie network.

Bill had a great knowledge of movies, especially some of the older films, and I recall we diligently checked out 'The Bill Collins Movie Show' every Saturday night on Channel 10.

Bill Collins with his wife Joan, 2008

Photo by News Ltd/Newspix

In 1963 Margaret Smith (later Court) became the first Australian woman to win a Wimbledon singles title

Wikipedia, photo Eric Koch

#28
FACT

In 2010, the *Herald Sun* newspaper of Melbourne, called Margaret Court the greatest female tennis player of all time. 'For sheer strength of performance and accomplishment there has never been a tennis player to match her. Court is one of only five tennis players all-time to win a multiple slam set in two disciplines, matching Roy Emerson, Martina Navratilova, Frank Sedgman, and Serena Williams.'

However, Margaret Court is the only one, in all of tennis history, to complete a multiple slam set in all three disciplines: singles, women's doubles, and mixed doubles.

She started playing tennis when she was only eight years old and when she turned 17 in 1960, she won the first of seven consecutive singles titles at the Australian Championships.

In the course of her brilliant career she won many titles and awards.

The world's longest straight stretch of railway track is in our own backyard. Were you sitting on the first Indian Pacific Trans-Australian Railway when it departed Sydney on 23 February 1970? The 4352 km journey includes the 478-km stretch across the Nullarbor Plain and arrives in Perth 75 hours later. Originally the train was limited to 144 passengers as this was the number that could be serviced by three sittings in the 48-seat dining car.

Four young girls sitting in a circle on an asphalt surface, playing with sheep knucklebones in a government school playground in 1954

Museum Victoria. Reg. No: MM 104110

In the Baby Boomer years, kids could make up a game with almost anything, including knuckle bones collected from the Sunday roast!

The games we played and the toys that we played with were not as expensive or as sophisticated as those of today. While the boys favoured marbles, brandy or chasey, the girls would either join in with us or play skippy, hop-scotch or knuklebones. Of course quite often we'd join in each other's games and I can vividly recall playing knucklebones with my sisters. I was thinking recently, how a set of five sheep's knucklebones, saved over a period of time from the Sunday roasts, could keep us all entertained for so many hours.

Cliff Young burst on to the Australian scene in 1983 when he won the Sydney to Melbourne Ultramarathon. It wasn't so much the win that captured our imagination, but the fact that he was 61 years old and not a professional runner or athlete.

Cliff was a potato farmer from Beech Forest in Victoria and at the beginning of the race he told the gathered media that his running experience amounted to chasing sheep around for two or three days in his gumboots.

Nobody really gave him a chance of winning, but Cliff's secret was he didn't need much sleep so he kept running all through the night while the other competitors slept. He took the lead after the first night and was never overtaken, winning the event by ten hours.

Cliff went on to compete in other marathons and remained a great media favourite until his death in 2003.

Cliff Young in training for the 875 km Ultramarathon, 1983

Photo by News Ltd/Newspix

'Because I said so, that's why'

dreamstime

I remember some of the things my mother used to say to me as a kid, like:

— 'Stop that crying or I'll give you something to really cry about!'
— 'Wait until your father gets home.'
— 'I don't care who started it.'
— 'She's the cat's mother.'
— 'It's a wigwam for a goose's bridle.'
— 'Not with the good scissors.'
— 'Beds are for sleeping in, not for jumping on.'
— 'I'm watching you, I've got eyes in the back of my head.'
— 'Eat your vegetables.'
— 'No one said life was supposed to be fair.'
— 'I don't know is not an answer.'
— 'If the wind changes, your face will stay like that.'
— 'Because I said so, that's why.'
— 'Don't sit so close to the TV, it'll ruin your eyes.'

And the one that I never quite appreciated until I got a bit older:

— 'If only you could put an old head on young shoulders.'

What are some of the things you can remember your Mum saying over and over again?

The milky would come every morning and exchange fresh bottles of milk for the empties

Photo by News Ltd/Newspix

Whenever I see the so-called celebrity chefs of today, I am reminded of my good friend Bernard King who was one of the wittiest and most talented TV personalities of the '70s and '80s.

I first met Bernard when he came to the Central Coast of NSW for some cooking demonstrations at our biggest shopping centre.

He always claimed that his career as a TV chef was more by accident than design: when he happened to invite 50 people to dinner and one of them was the host of the ABC program 'Woman's World'. She loved his food so much she immediately organised a cooking spot for him on the show, and he never looked back.

Remember when you would be woken each morning to the sound of clinking glass bottles as the milky delivered fresh milk to your home?

It was a daily ritual that lasted right through my childhood and up until the early '80s. Indeed many milkies even continued to use the old horse and cart for the regular delivery until the early '70s at least.

Some people may still recall milk being delivered in a billy, which had been put out for the milkman, the milk ladelled out from large milk urns.

Perhaps as we get older our memories begin to play tricks on us, but somehow I seem to remember that milk back then was creamier, especially if you were the first to remove the silver foil lid and got to pour the fresh milk from the bottle on your corn flakes first.

As the '70s progressed Bernard turned up on a host of TV programs, culminating in his own 30-minute cooking show 'King's Kitchen'. He pioneered the TV advertorial and by the early '80s he was reportedly earning 5 million dollars a year from sponsorship deals, licensing arrangements, a signature range of herbs and spices, and wide-ranging media commitments.

Sadly, in later years, Bernard struggled financially, and when he died in 2002 he was almost penniless.

Ita Buttrose and Bernard King at the Melbourne Cup, 1982. Bernard was a great talent, well before his time

Photo by News Ltd/Newspix

Alex Inns shared a photo of something he has carefully kept from his childhood, something that is very collectable now, a Skippy plate. Thanks Alex!

Courtesy of Alex Inns

Ahh yes, 'Skippy the Bush Kangaroo'! It originally ran from 1966 to 1968 on Channel 9 and told the adventures of a young boy and his intelligent pet kangaroo, Skippy, and the various visitors to the fictitious Waratah National Park in Duffy's Forest, near Sydney.

Ed Deveraux, Ken James, Tony Bonner and Garry Pankhurst were the stars of the program, along with Skippy of course, who was played by at least nine kangaroos.

The Nine Network repeated the series several times after Australian television switched to colour transmission in 1975 and it's probably still being played by one of the digital channels.

The Beatles arrived in Sydney on the morning of 11 June 1964 to begin their much awaited Australian tour.

They were greeted, as they would be throughout the entire tour, by thousands of screaming fans and a horde of eager journalists and cameramen.

Ken Brodziak was the man behind the tour and as luck would have it, had booked the group for appearances before they became so famous. Legend has it that the contract was never actually signed, but Brian Epstein, the Beatles manager, honoured the original verbal agreement and also allowed a punishing schedule for the band. In Adelaide, Melbourne, Sydney and Brisbane — with a lightning side trip to New Zealand — the Beatles were playing two shows a night, at 6pm and 8pm, often on consecutive days.

Scenes of mayhem greeted the band wherever they went, from the mass turnout in Adelaide to the crowd around their Melbourne hotel that brought the CBD to a grinding halt.

Promoter Michael Gudinski was too young to be allowed to go to their sold-out shows at Festival Hall, but remembers well the impact the visit had on his hometown. In all his years of bringing some of the biggest acts in the world to Australia, he says he has still never seen anything like it.

Scenes of mayhem during the Beatles 1964 tour

Photo by News Ltd/Newspix

Who remembers fish 'n' chips with salt and vinegar, wrapped in yesterday's newspaper?

Andrew Heslop, Commentator, MC and Community Advocate has shared this photo and some memories about growing up:

> Vinegar was once on the counter at every fish and chip shop in the country. The bottle provided a thin stream of vinegar through a tiny hole in the top, right on to your steaming fish and chips.
>
> With the advent of multinational fast food chains, the corner 'fish and chips' shops – many owned by hard working first-generation migrants – have closed.
>
> My favourite is still open – Sotos on Semaphore Road down near the beach in Adelaide. Many happy memories of being there with my grandparents during summer and taking our meal across to the (now closed) sideshows and summer carnival. Happy days!

Fish 'n' chips tasted much better when they were wrapped in yesterday's newspaper

Courtesy of Andrew Heslop

#29
FACT

'Mr. Squiggle', a puppet with a pencil for a nose, was Australia's longest-running television program. Created by Norman Hetherington and screened on the ABC for 40 years, Mr. Squiggle visited his friends by rocket from his home on the moon, and aided by a human would draw pictures based on squiggles sent in by adoring children across the nation.

Typing pools were noisy work environments

Photo by Jim Fenwick/Newspix

There was a time, not that long ago, when girls in their teens were put into a commercial stream at high school and were taught typing and how to keep books.

Many went on to secretarial courses where they were also taught shorthand and how to file before joining the workforce.

For many companies, filing was crucial as duplicate documents weren't always kept as backups. Before computers were widely used, typing was a valuable skill in the workforce. Bigger companies had typing pools and these women were expected to be quick and accurate.

When computers came along they created a cheaper and more efficient environment for workers to do their own typing. Though for executives and others in top-end jobs, a personal assistant will still take care of correspondence and typing needs.

Remember the little owner operated shops in your suburb or town?

Courtesy of Roger Ray

This scene is sadly replicated today in almost every city and town around Australia.

The derelict remains of an old shop building that was once a thriving little business and, most likely, the livelihood of its owner and employees. I remember as a kid there were plenty of small shops like this, little hardware shops, grain and fodder stores, butchers' shops, grocery stores and delis to name a few, around in every suburb. Sadly today they are all disappearing, along with personal service.

Back in the day you could purchase only what you needed, nothing was pre-packaged, everything came in a big cardboard box or tin, which could then be counted or weighed out to the amount you wanted.

Remember the Graeme Thorne kidnapping in 1960?

Graeme's father, Bazil Thorne, had won £100 000 (equivalent to about $6 million in today's value) in the Opera House lottery on 1 June. There was no option of privacy for lottery winners in those days, so the details of Mr Thorne's lottery win were published on the front pages of Sydney newspapers.

On 7 July, Graeme was kidnapped while on his way to school. The crime caused massive shock at the time all around Australia and was the first known kidnapping for ransom in Australian history. I can recall how my parents were absolutely horrified that a child would be kidnapped in Australia.

On 16 August, Graeme Thorne's body was discovered in Seaforth in Sydney, wrapped in a blue tartan rug. Graeme was still wearing his school uniform. Stephen Bradley was eventually arrested for the kidnap and murder, and sentenced to life imprisonment.

Graeme's kidnapping and horrific murder was national news

Photo by News Ltd/Newspix

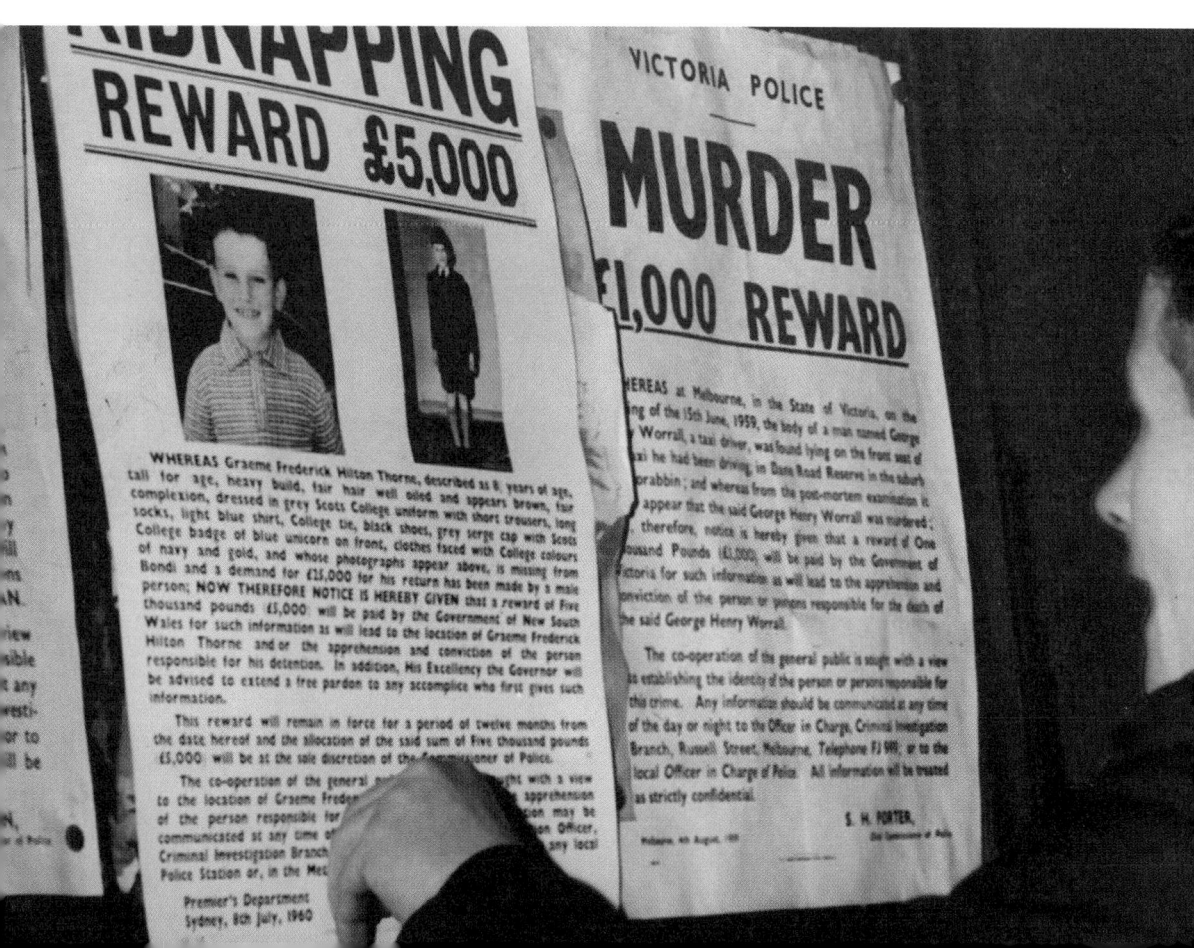

There was a time when newspaper kiosks or booths were dotted around the streets of the CBD in most cities.

There may be a few remaining, but the rise and rise of online newspapers has seen their gradual demise.

The kiosks usually carried the latest edition of the city dailies and a wide range of magazines. I remember too when they sold cigarettes, but I think that was stopped when more stringent laws were passed regarding the sale of smokes to minors. I believe the last paper I purchased from a little kiosk was possibly in the early 1990s.

A newspaper kiosk in Adelaide. There were many of these small booths around Australian cities selling newspapers and magazines

Photo by News Ltd/Newspix

Laurene and Kim Bell shared a memory: 'Does anyone remember playing elastics at school?'

I first saw the game when I moved from the bush to Adelaide and went to primary school.

It was a game that the girls mainly played at recess and lunch.

You needed three girls, two to hold the elastic and the other one to complete their routine in the middle of the elastic; the one doing the routine jumps into the middle of the elastics and performs a series of jumping over and onto the elastic. It starts off with the elastics on the ground around the ankles of the two girls holding it and then as that part of the routine is completed by the girl in the middle the elastics is moved up to the knees and then the waist and so on.

Does anyone remember playing elastics at school? Any experts out there?

ARW

Footballer Ron Barrassi tries his hand at tenpin bowling, 1961

Photo by News Ltd/Newspix

Tenpin bowling has been around in Australia since the early 1900s, but when the automatic pinsetting machinery became available in the '60s the popularity of the game exploded.

The first fully automatic centre opened in Hurstville, Sydney in 1960 and reached Melbourne and other Australian cities and towns by 1961.

Suddenly everyone was tenpin bowling – leagues were established all over the country and I recall playing for the first time in about 1963 as a member of the Australian Postal Institute team.

The sport became so popular there was a tenpin bowling comp broadcast live on TV on a Saturday afternoon back in the '80s.

The game is still very popular today! Did you ever go tenpin bowling when it was all the rage back in the '60s?

Who still uses their CorningWare dishes?

Wikipedia

CorningWare was originally a brand name for a unique pyroceramic glass cookware, and was first introduced in 1958 by Corning Glass Works. CorningWare was a great discovery as it could be used directly on the stovetop.

The original range featured the blue 'Cornflower' pattern and according to Wikipedia more than 750 million pieces of CorningWare's range/oven-to-table service have been manufactured since its inception.

We still have the casserole dishes and a coffee pot somewhere, I think.

#30
FACT

Macramé. What household didn't have a cream or brown plant hanger or wall hanging made from this wonderful technique of decorative knotting? Originating in the 13th century, and a common pastime for sailors, it made a comeback in the 1970s after centuries of obscurity. It was a common school project during that time and remains popular today.

The one and only J.O.K

Photo by Al Pascoe/Newspix

Johnny O'Keefe was a lovable larrikin who became Australia's first successful rock 'n' roll singer in the mid-1950s.

Known either as J.O.K. or 'The Wild One', he had been singing for a number of years on stage in various groups. Once he saw Bill Haley and the Comets performing 'Rock Around the Clock' in the film of the same name, he immediately knew that he would become a rock singer.

He chased his dream relentlessly and became the first Australian artist to make the local Top 40 charts and the first Australian rock 'n' roll performer to tour the US. He had 29 Top 40 hits in Australia between 1959 and 1974, a number of EPs and successful LPs.

Davy Crockett's coonskin hat

Courtesy of Valerie O'Donaghue

Davy Crockett was a boyhood hero of mine as I'm sure was for many boys and girls who grew up in the '50s.

My first recollection of my hero I think might have been the song, 'The Ballad of Davy Crockett', which came from the American TV series first broadcast there in 1954. We didn't have TV in Australia at that time, but I think there might have been a radio serial produced here. The Walt Disney movie followed in 1955 and although we never had the marketing push of film paraphernalia back then, I really wanted a coonskin hat. Never ever got one though, might have been too expensive for the Father Christmas who came to our place!

Fess Parker was a good Davy Crockett and I think there might have been a couple of films where he played the hero. I never took to John Wayne as DC in *The Alamo* though, which probably came out in the '60s.

The Davy Crockett craze pretty much ended by the early '60s.

Did you have a Davy Crockett coonskin hat as a kid?

Remember 'Kingswood Country', the Australian sitcom that screened from 1980 to 1984 on Channel 7?

Some of Ted Bullpit's sayings included: 'The Kingswood! You're not taking the Kingswood!', 'Bloody woman!', 'Pickle me grandmother!' and 'Don't "Dad" me, I'm your father!'

Ted was the main character; he was a bigoted white Australian World War II veteran who loved his greyhounds, his garden statue of Neville the Aboriginal and his chair in front of the telly. He worshipped his Holden Kingswood and hated the 'bloody' nuns.

The show centred on the conflict between the sexist and racist Ted and his progressive children with his poor, long- suffering wife Thelma, stuck in the middle.

His daughter's husband, Bruno, was the son of Italian immigrants and Ted objected to him completely, referring to him as 'that bloody wog'.

I don't know if you could play it on TV these days, very politically incorrect, but it was real Aussie humour and a very funny show!

Ross Higgins as Ted Bullpit and Lex Marinos as his son-in-law, Bruno, in a scene from the weekly TV show 'Kingswood Country'

Photo by News Ltd/Newspix

WE CAME IN PEACE FOR ALL MANKIND

THIS IS TO CERTIFY THAT

DAVID JOHN MADLEY

WAS ON THE EARTH WHEN MAN FIRST SET FOOT ON THE MOON 21st JULY 1969 A.D.

THE NEWS

NWS channel 9

EDWIN E. ALDRIN ASTRONAUT

MICHAEL COLLINS ASTRONAUT

NEIL A. ARMSTRONG ASTRONAUT

An official moon-landing certificate

Courtesy of David J Madley

David J Madley sent me this photo that certainly brought back a few memories: 'Does anybody remember these 'official' certificates from Channel 9 and *The Newspaper* from 1969? Did you get yours? I lost mine a looooong time ago.

Mark Gerry Eubel shared this photo and some memories:

Here is a photo of my 1965 PYE PEDIGREE black and white TV which was an iconic set back in the 1960s and '70s. How many people remember watching 'Homicide' on one of these back in the day? This one still works fine and is set up for free-to-air so I can watch all the shopping channels and ads in 'living black and white'.

I bought my first black and white television after I'd moved away from home in about 1968. We kept it until colour TV arrived in the 1970s. Watched such programs as 'Cop Shop', 'Homicide', 'Number 96', 'The Box' and 'Ask the Leyland Brothers', etc, etc.

Can you remember what your first TV set was?

One of the most popular black and white TV sets in the 1960s

Courtesy of Mark Gerry Eubel

#31
FACT

Remember Margot Fonteyn and Rudolf Nureyev? They joined the Australian Ballet as guest artists in Peggy van Praagh's *Swan Lake* and *Giselle* in 1964 and took audiences by storm. Nureyev toured many times with the Australian Ballet and in 1972 directed *Don Quixote* in Melbourne, one of the most acclaimed ballet films ever made.

Once upon a time, the little corner shop was such an important part of any neighbourhood

Courtesy of Chris Adams

Chris Adams shared this photo:

Anybody remember the 1960s and the corner shop where you could buy all your daily necessities, with the old red phone booth and post bx out the front?

Thanks Chris. What a great photo and some sensational memories.

Before the large suburban shopping centres we had lots of little independently run corner stores and shops. Four Square or Serv-Wel, run by families. Most had a lolly counter, where sixpence would get you a big brown paper bag of assorted favourites. When you went with Mum to the shop there were always some broken biscuits in the biscuit tin for the kids and many of the greengrocers had a truck for deliveries or an old bus that they'd drive.

Attendants 'servicing' an EH Holden motor car at a service station in Bulleen. The attendants are cleaning the windsreen and checking the motor and tyre pressure

Museum Victoria. Reg. No: MM 55244

It seems like a lifetime ago when you could drive into a petrol station and ask the petrol pump attendant to 'fill her up please'.

There was a time when bowser boys filled up our cars, washed the windscreen, checked the oil and tyres and performed some of the minor jobs like fixing the windscreen wipers.

Many of the petrol stations then were small independent operators that also had a mechanical workshop where they could service and maintain your car – assistance they provided on the driveway was an important part of their ongoing business. Many of the petrol pump attendants were indentured to the business, learning their trade as a mechanic, so it was all part of their apprenticeship. Sadly they were replaced by self-service petrol pumps.

Remember the night that Molly died in 'A Country Practice'?

A Country Practice was one of the longest running soapies ever made in Australia and ran on Channel 7 for 1058 episodes – from 18 November 1981 to 22 November 1993.

The most famous episode of course was the death of Molly Jones, played by Anne Tenney. Legend has it that the Molly's death storyline was originally written for an 11-week script, but producers realised that her death was proposed in a week where there were no ratings so they stretched it out for two extra episodes, hence the storyline lasted 13 weeks, making it one of the longest death scene in TV history.

It was a very effective episode though and rates apparently as one of the highest rating episodes in the series with 2.2 million viewers.

Molly Jones fighting leukaemia in a scene from 'A Country Practice'

Photo by News Ltd/Newspix

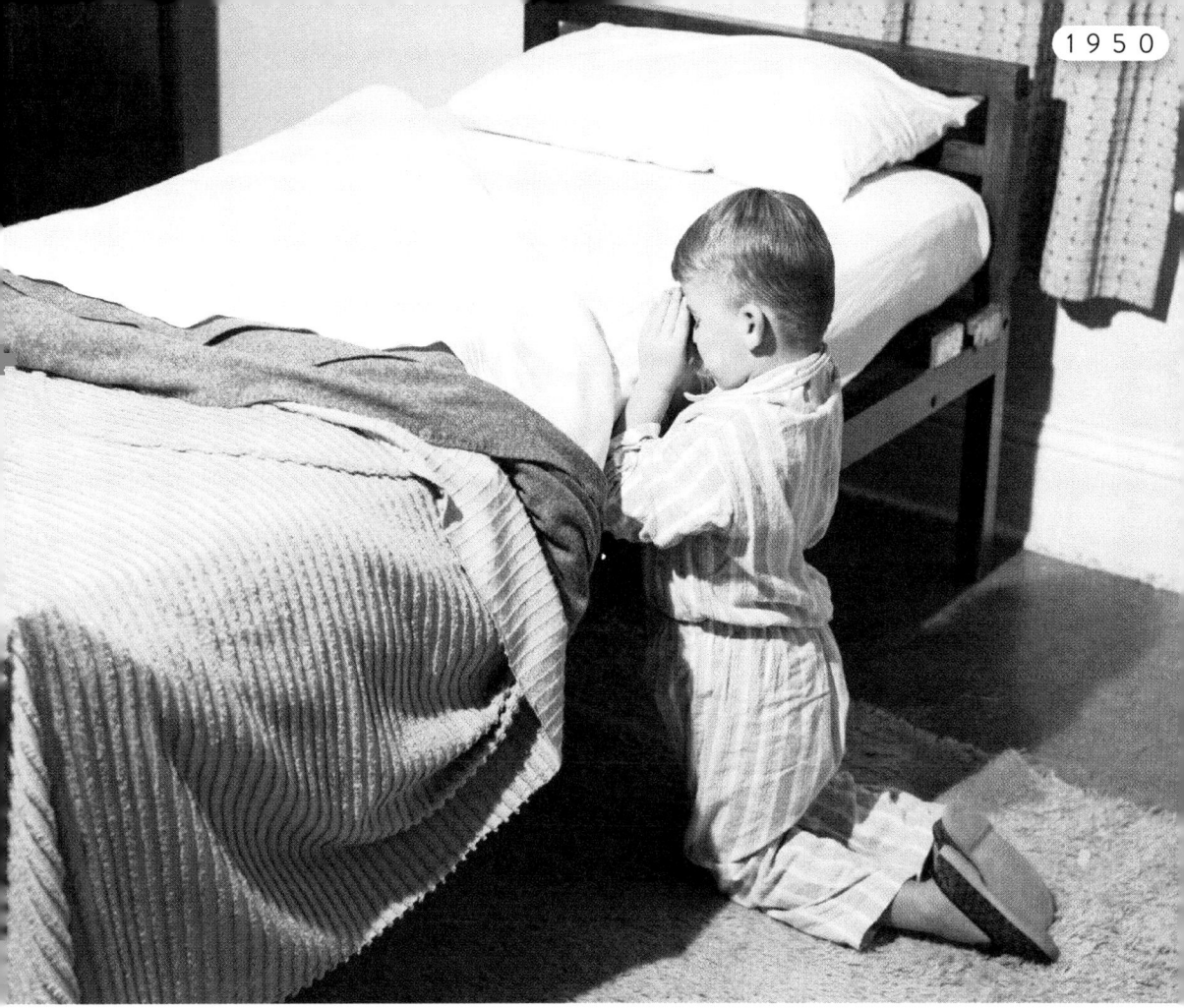

A child saying his prayers before bedtime in the 1950s

Photo by News Ltd/Newspix

Religion seemed to play a much bigger role in the '50s and '60s, and almost everyone from our neighbourhood went to church on Sunday.

Throughout my childhood years in the '50s, religion was something that everyone had. We were an Irish Catholic family so every Sunday morning it was off to Mass. The women were required to cover their heads, while the men hung their hats in the vestibule. We said the rosary as a family every night and as children, we said our prayers before jumping into bed.

Almost everyone back then believed that children needed some religious teaching as the basis of moral values and character. The maintenance of 'Christian standards' were seen as the only secure means of preventing juvenile delinquency.

#32
FACT

In a 1985 victory for Aboriginal land rights, the Federal Government of the day announced that it would return Uluru to its traditional owners on the condition that the Kata Tjuta National Park be leased back to the federal parks service for 99 years. Despite hysterical fears that Australians would be locked out of the Park, nearly 300 000 tourists visited the site in 2013 alone!

Playing card games ... We used to love 'Old Maid'

Pinterest

Can you recall some of the games we used to play indoors as kids in the '50s and '60s?

Do you remember playing 'Old Maid'? Probably wouldn't be encouraged these days as it portrayed single, unmarried women as unattractive spinsters who were to be avoided.

We also played knucklebones (not plastic ones but with the real bones), Ludo, Chinese Checkers, Snakes and Ladders, Tiddley Winks, Barrel of Monkeys, Monopoly and Pick-Up Sticks. Other card games were Snap, Rummy, someone recalled Hearts (not sure what that was about), Crazy Eights and, I also seem to recall, something called Sevens.

I also remember my Grandma trying to teach us how to play 500s or Euchre.

It seems like such a long time ago since I sat down and played a card or board game.

What are some of your memories of sitting around the kitchen table with the family, having fun playing games?

Elliot broke his own records many times

Photo by News Ltd/Newspix

How proud Australia was in the late 1950s and early 1960s of Herb Elliot, one of the greatest athletes of the time. He was one of the world's truly great middle-distance runners and during his short but brilliant career, broke the four-minute barrier for the mile no less than 17 times. At the 1960 Olympics, he won the gold medal for the 1500-metre event and in doing so, bettered his own world record time of 3:35.6.

He was one of the bearers of the Olympic Torch at the opening ceremony of the Olympic Games in Sydney in 2000, and entered the stadium for the final segment before the lighting of the Olympic Flame.

Back in the day, many houses had an outside lavatory (it was never called a toilet then). Before sewage pipes were laid across the suburbs and major country towns, men would collect tins of human waste at night. They would empty the waste into a larger tin and place the newly emptied tin, back inside the thunderbox.

These men were known as nightmen, or in some places, dunnymen, and it was their job to get rid of waste. Apparently at the time, this waste, called nightsoil, was used as fertiliser on market gardens.

I remember as a small child we lived in a house that had a pan toilet. If the nightman was running late and you were using the toilet first thing in the morning, you would have to quickly get off if you heard him coming.

The job is now obsolete but up until the '50s and '60s the 'nightman' would call by and replace the full lavatory pan in many suburban and country areas around Australia

Photo by News Ltd/Newspix

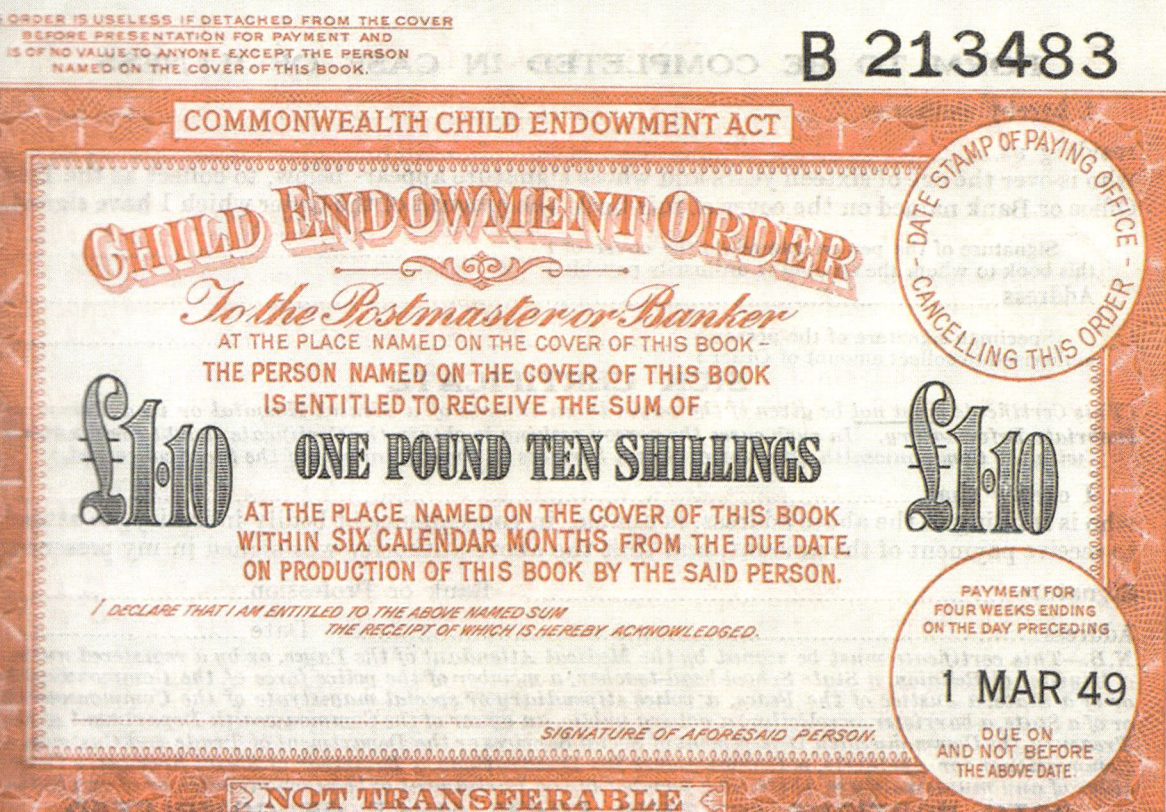

Child Endowment was a blessing to families when first introduced in the 1940s and 1950s

Courtesy of Downies Auctions

Remember when your Mum went to the Post Office to collect her 'Child Endowment'?

Child endowment was first introduced in Australia in the 1940s and was paid direct to the mother at a flat rate of five shillings per week for each child after the first under the age of 16 years.

Child endowment was not means tested and there was no tax on it either. To receive the benefit a child had to be under 16. The parent and child had to have been born in Australia or a resident for 12 months immediately prior to the claim.

The Child Endowment Act changed in 1950 so a first child aged under 16 years received five shillings and for the second and each additional child continued at 10 shillings per week. Obviously this change was popular among larger families.

The name Greg Norman, 'The Great White Shark', is synonymous with Australian golf.

He did not start playing until he was about 15, but was an absolute natural from the very start. Within 18 months of picking up a golf club he went from a handicap of 27 to scratch.

Greg Norman turned professional in 1976 and earned his first major victory that very same year at the Grange Golf Club in Adelaide. He, of course, went on to win many major titles and finished the season on top of the ranking list on seven occasions; 1986, 1987, 1989, 1990, 1995, 1996 and 1997.

In 2007, 'The Shark' was elevated to 'Legend' status in the Sport Australia Hall of Fame.

He continues to play competition golf, but is also involved in running Great White Shark Enterprises, a multi-national corporation which is focused around golf, golf-course design and the golfing lifestyle.

One of Australia's best-known faces

Wikipedia, photo Ted Van Pelt

Some nights we'd go 'window shopping', which was especially exciting during Christmas

Courtesy of Frank and Elaine Hall

I recall as a family we would go 'window shopping'. I think it was something my mother loved to do and she would take us into the city, mainly in the early evening when all the shops were closed, just to see the latest merchandise.

We would amble along the street looking at clothes, or at Christmas

#33
FACT

Were you or someone you know a Nasho? 800 000 men registered for National Service, as well as those whose names were drawn from a 'birthday ballot'. The first Nasho's birthdate was drawn from a lottery barrel in 1965 and 64 000 more would be called up to the army until the scheme ended in 1972. Many spent their time in army barracks in Australia, but many 'Nashos' fought and died in Vietnam.

time, the toys, and point out what we did or did not like. Seeing this photo of a shopping strip, taken back in 1966, immediately took me back to those more innocent, unhurried times when even a simple stroll past the big department stores could be a wonderful experience.

Going to school in the '50 and '60s we used to salute the flag (the Union Jack) once every week and sing 'God Save the Queen'.

We'd all stand to attention, put our hand on our chest and recite 'I am an Australian. I love my country. I salute her flag. I honour her Queen. I promise to obey her laws.' Then we would march into classes to the sound of our own school fife and drum band.

Do you remember doing that too?

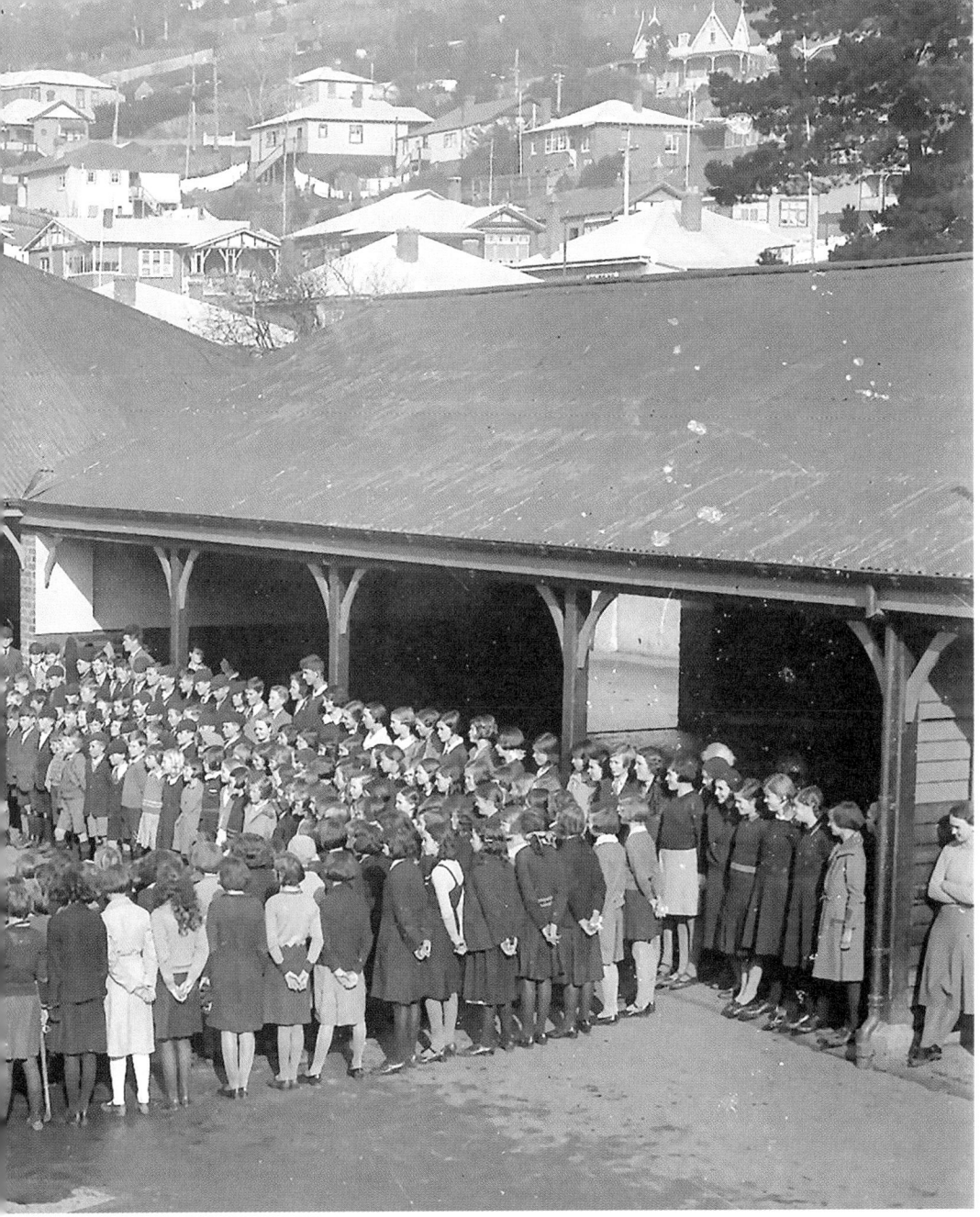

Once a week we would raise the flag at school,
salute and recite the loyal affirmation

Photo by News Ltd/Newspix

World Series Cricket had rather humble beginnings. The first so-called 'Supertest' between the Australians and the West Indians began at VFL Park in Melbourne on 2 December 1977.

The cricket was excellent, but the crowds were pretty thin on the ground, and it would take some time before Australians accepted this new form of the old game.

The formation of the new game was driven in part by Kerry Packer, who wanted to secure the exclusive broadcasting rights to Australian cricket, held by the ABC. The other driver was that players felt that they were not being paid enough to make a living from cricket.

Between 1977 and 1979 Packer secretly signed agreements with leading Australian, English, South African, Pakistani and West Indian players. These included Australian captain Greg Chappell, fast bowler Denis Lillee and England captain Tony Greig. And by doing so he set up his own series.

Kerry Packer's Australian team at Moorabbin Oval, Melbourne, 1977

Photo by News Ltd/Newspix

I often ask people what they remember most about growing up in Australia from the '50s to the '80s.

Of course I get all sorts of answers, and people from different states will sometimes recall totally diverse experiences. But there are a number of things that obviously happened right across this country that almost everyone remembers: such as playing backyard, street or beach cricket with friends or neighbours at some stage of their childhood.

The rules of the game varied widely, but the principle remained the same – to get the batsman out.

There may have been teams, or perhaps the players would just take turns at batting and there was often no need to actually score runs.

Tennis balls were quite acceptable as they're more readily available and didn't hurt as much if you happen to get hit.

The pitch could be any length and just needed to be reasonably flat.

The wicket could be anything at all really, a chair, rubbish bin, wooden crate, 44-gallon drum or any convenient object. You could have something to represent a wicket at the non-strikers end but it's not essential.

And that's it really. Oh, and a whole lot of kids, the more the merrier.

Backyard cricket, all you needed was something to act as a set of stumps, a bat and a ball and a whole lot of kids

Photo by Alan Funnell/Newspix

217

The typical comfy lounge room in suburban
Australian homes in the 1970s

Courtesy of David J Madley

David J Madley shared a photo that will bring back lots of memories I'm sure: 'This was my grandparents lounge room at their home, circa early '70s.'

The colours of burnt orange and brown were the height of impeccable taste at the time. There was the Australian made TV set, a gas/oil heater, the tray table and the ash tray (because almost everybody smoked inside), and the wall mural. Some lounge rooms may have featured the painting of the 'Green Chinese Girl' or a large wooden knife and fork set, or perhaps even three flying ducks.

The TV would have been black and white of course because colour TV didn't arrive until early 1975. I love this photo – the main difference to our place was the wallpaper mural and we had the wooden clock on the wall that chimed every hour! Great pic, lots of memories there.

#34

FACT

Fondue was central to many Australian dinner parties in the 1970s. Guests would drink claret and chat around a pot of molten cheese, into which they dipped all kinds of morsels. The fondue fad may have passed, but fondue sets – usually bright orange – have become vintage collectables.

'Up There Cazaly', inspired by the brilliant high-flying marking abilities of St Kilda's Roy Cazaly

Wikipedia

'Up There Cazaly' was a song recorded in 1979 by the Two Man Band, Mike Brady and Peter Sullivan, and was inspired by the spectacular marks taken by players in Aussie Rules football.

'Cazaly' was Roy Cazaly, who played football from 1909 to 1927 for St Kilda and South Melbourne. He was famous for his brilliant marking ability. According to legend he could mark and turn in mid-air, land and in a few strides send forward a long accurate drop-kick or stab-pass. His team mates' constant cry, 'Up there Cazaly', was taken up by the crowds and later became the inspiration for the best-selling song. It was later used by Channel 7 to introduce the 'live' telecast of games and is often featured in pre-match entertainment at the AFL Grand Final.

1951

I'm sure it's one of the most enduring memories we all have about school!

In the early 1950s, the Australian Government introduced a scheme for school children to receive free milk. I think the idea was to ensure that all Australian children were getting fresh milk and a good dose of calcium each day.

The idea might have been fine, but in practice there were a few problems. The truck would normally drop the milk off at about 9.30am and recess wasn't until 10.45am (from memory) and on a hot summer's day the milk would go off. No refrigeration was available and the teacher made you drink the milk, off or not.

Many people over 50 still blame the school milk program for the fact that they're unable to stomach a milk drink to this day.

The old school pencil sharpener. I can still smell the shavings!

Pinterest

At school we had an old manual pencil sharpener out in front of the classroom, which was attached to the teacher's desk.

Teachers hated blunt pencils and I can remember, on more than one occasion, being hauled out in front of the class and instructed to sharpen my pencil and get back to finishing my school work.

Funny how the memory of something like that can trigger other memories too, like the smell of the pencil shavings that collected in the old sharpener, the smell too of schoolbooks in the big stationary cupboards and the ink in inkwells being topped up on Mondays by the ink monitor.

These days, of course, pencil sharpeners are battery operated and pencils and pens are used less and less as classrooms become digital.

I wonder how many kids today would have used one of these?

Helping Australian children grow strong bones

Photo by Al Pascoe/Newspix

A lot of things passed as art in the post-war Australia of the '50s and '60s.

Remember the 'Flying Ducks', which were very popular as a decoration on the kitchen wall? We never had the ducks at home, but I do remember plenty of houses where you would see them on the wall, mainly in the kitchen and sometimes in the lounge.

They are now apparently quite valuable, and if they're the 'Beswick Flying Ducks (Mallard) Wall Plaques', they can fetch up to $1000 or so.

My mother also had a 'Toby' jug, which we thought was very valuable. It turned out to be a copy and not the real deal, but it still has lots of sentimental value!

I have lots of flying ducks on my walls. This is my Beswick set

Courtesy of Victoria Blanch Robinson

#35
FACT

My shout.
The Cascade brewery in Tasmania is Australia's oldest continuously operating brewery. But we drink half as much beer as we did in the 1970s, and beer consumption is at its lowest level since 1945.

The Beast, John Laws, surrounded by Beauty!

Photo by News Ltd/Newspix

There are a few faces you may remember here from your TV screen, circa 1970s.

Remember 'Beauty And The Beast'? It was a panel show first launched by the Seven Network in 1964. The basic premise was to pit a sardonic or sometimes chauvinistic host ('the beast') against a panel of females ('the beauties'), who would respond to viewers' pressing, or not so pressing, issues.

Eric Baume was the first 'beast', and others to follow after his death included Stuart Wagstaff, Rex Mossop, John Laws and Alwyn Kurts.

The original version of Beauty And The Beast last appeared in 1973. In 1982 the format was revived by two rival networks at the same time. The Seven Network revival was headed by Derryn Hinch, while John Laws reprised his role as 'beast' for Network Ten's version. Laws was later replaced by Clive Robertson.

Come on everybody, it's time for **Chocolate Crackles**

Preparing chocolate bubble cakes – a useful life-long skill to have!

Courtesy of Copha, a registered trademark of Peerless Foods Pty Ltd

Remember home economics, taught in schools back in the '50s and maybe even up to the '80s?

Back in the day, boys were never taught this subject because it was already decided that girls would be the home makers and boys would be the bread winners ... just the way it was back then!

A Home Ec teacher, explains that 'Home Economics isn't just about baking and sewing; it teaches the fundamental principals of food buying and the psychology of clothing.' And that 'Home economics training teaches ways of developing democratic practices within the home and anyone who's going to be married and a homemaker would be foolish NOT to take Home Economics!'

When I left home at age 20, I couldn't cook (still pretty hopeless), would not have had a clue about mending or sewing, and had very little experience of cleaning or washing clothes. Why did they think back then that boys did not need to learn these things?

What are your memories of home economics at school?

I'm guessing that a lot of people who grew up in the '60s and '70s would remember watching 'H.R. Pufnstuf'.

The story revolved around Jimmy's adventures on Living Island and trying to save Freddie, his talking flute, from ending up in Witchiepoo's clutches. It aired originally on Saturday mornings on Channel 9 as part of 'The Wacky Quack Show' and the movie version featured singer, Mama Cass, in her only film role.

As far as I remember Pufnstuf was the friendly dragon and mayor, who lived in the cave on Living Island – it was the only place on the whole island where Whitchiepoo's spells didn't work. Everything on the island was alive of course, including all the trees and rocks and they were all puppets. If my memory is right, many of the characters had the voices of famous movie stars, including some of the biggest names of the era, such as John Wayne.

What are your memories of Pufnstuf?

'Pufnstuf' was a children's TV show from the '60s which we used to watch on Saturday mornings

Wikipedia

Hobbytex took off in the '70s. I remember my wife doing this with our children

Courtesy of Michelle Brewer

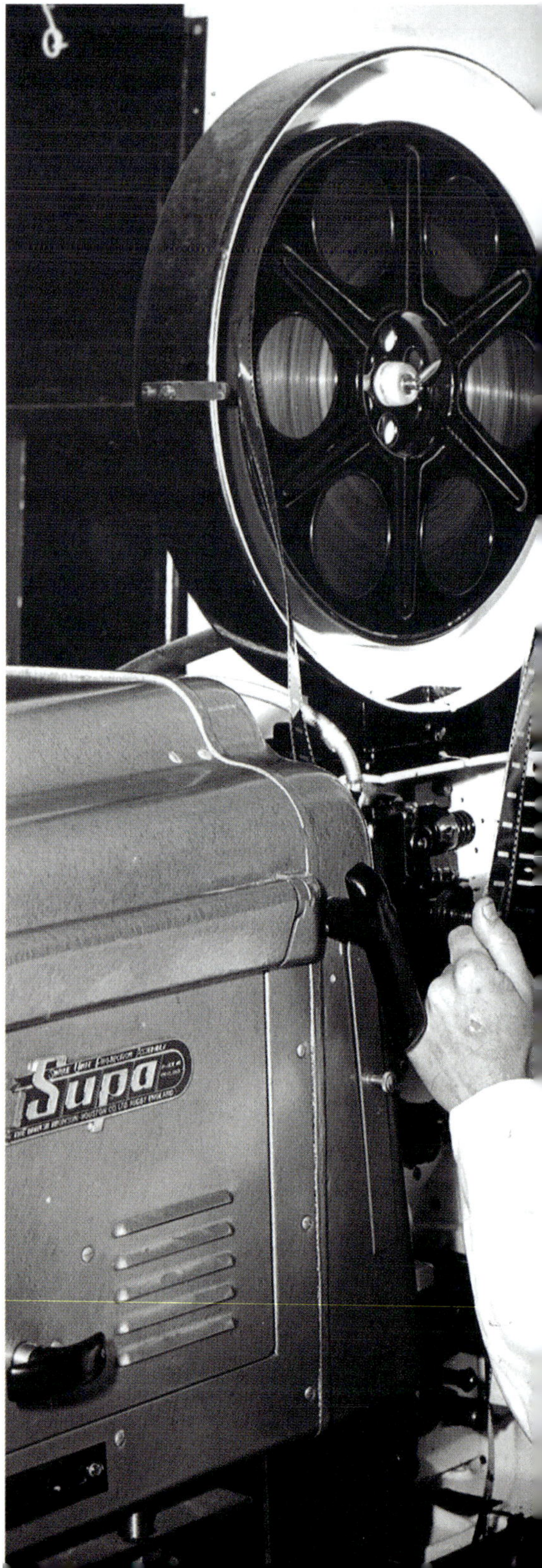

Michelle Brewer shared a photo:

Saw this in an Op Shop in the city on Wednesday. Brought back memories of the '70s when Hobbytex was the craze. Even remember going to classes with friends as a child learning to do it.

I had nearly forgotten about Hobbytex. It was an Australian company that first started in about 1968. Haven't heard much about them since the '80s and not sure whether they are still going.

As far as I can remember, it was like fabric paint in a ball-point tube and you could buy the patterns which you then painted!

There were t-shirts, doileys, tablecloths and all sorts of things you could make patterned with Hobbytex.

Remember Hobbytex at all?

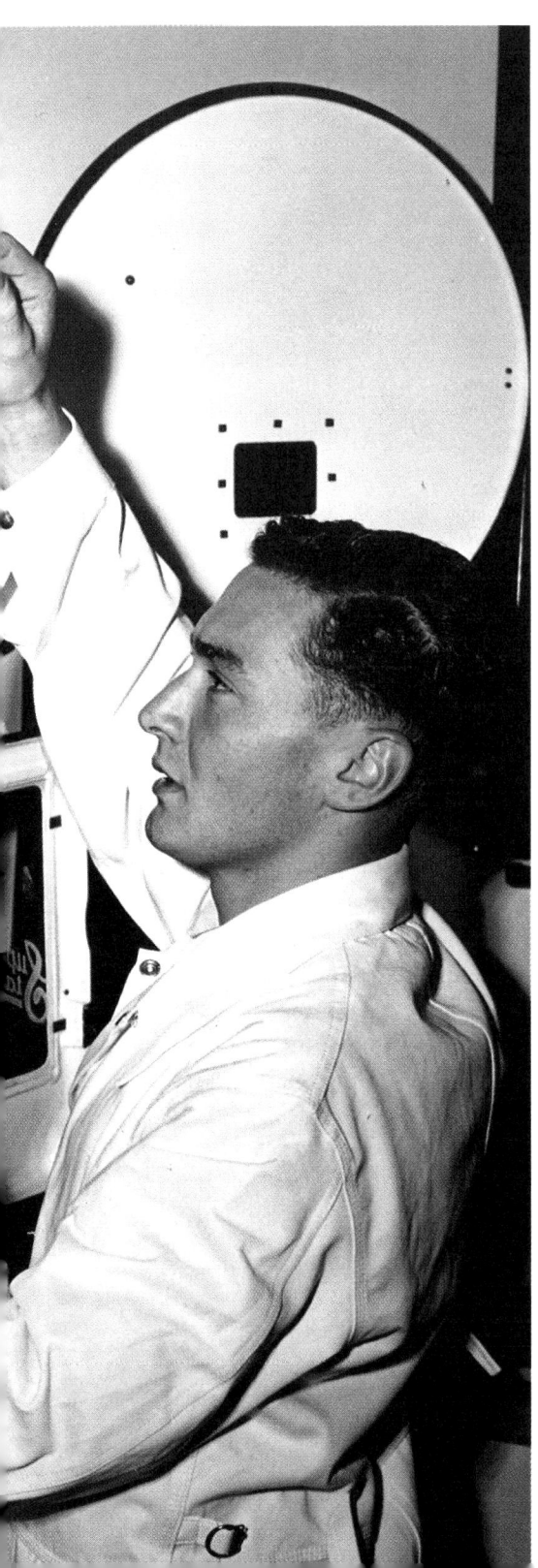

Remember when the film would break at the pictures?

I'm thinking back to those Saturday afternoon matinees when right in the middle of a John Wayne cowboy flick, the screen would suddenly go white and the theatre would break out with cat calls, jeers and boos. Back then, projectionists changed film reels by hand and had to know how to cut and splice the footage whenever it broke. It was also up to the projectionist to know when to change over projectors as films were never on just one reel.

This is another job that's been phased out through digital film technology. It has allowed cinemas to operate with fewer staff, as one person is no longer required to watch each and every minute of the movie to make sure it runs smoothly.

In fact, these days it's more than likely that the person selling the tickets and serving in the candy bar is also the person to start the movie program. Sometimes nowadays one or two people can run the entire theatre. There was a time when there was a ticket seller, candy bar attendants, people to check and take your tickets, half a dozen ushers or usherettes, the projectionist and a manager on duty.

A movie projectionist – another job that has been phased out over time

Photo by News Ltd/Newspix

We had to learn cursive writing at school

dreamstime

A recent newspaper article reported 'the once art of penmanship and handwriting, a skill developed through endless practice is disappearing from secondary schools, leaving many senior students unable to write quickly or fluently'.

Teachers blame the increasing use of computers throughout society. Some say that illegible handwriting is becoming so problematic that lots of students cannot even read their own writing!

Cursive handwriting is still taught in primary school, but when students reach high school then tend to drop the cursive style and begin printing in a very childlike hand.

Texting is also undermining the English language itself. Nowadays, I almost need a translator to decipher some of the text messages I receive from younger colleagues!

Technology, it seems, has a lot to answer for!

Remember when rock 'n' roll first came to Australia? There have been many debates and arguments about the origins of rock music, but I think most people agree that the first popular song to be genuinely recognised as rock 'n' roll was Bill Haley and the Comets, 'Rock Around the Clock'.

Bill had previously been a country music performer and was a champion yodeller, but changed musical direction to a new sound which would eventually become known as 'rock 'n' roll'.

The manager of Wests Theatre in Adelaide with the police trying to control the crowd at the first screening of the film, *Rock Around the Clock*

Photo by News Ltd/Newspix

The Comets, with Bill as lead singer, had nine singles in the Top 20 during the 1950s, the biggest in 1953, being 'Rock Around the Clock'.

Sales of 'Rock Around the Clock' started slowly but eventually sold an estimated 25 million copies (according to the *Guinness Book of World Records*) around the world. The reason it took so long for it to be recognised is probably due to its use in the soundtrack of the film, *Blackboard Jungle*, which was released in 1956. The song was re-released to coincide with the film, and rose to the top of the American music charts that summer – staying there for eight weeks, the first rock and roll record to do so.

#36
FACT

Nintendo's first 'Game Boy' device was released in 1989 and was a hugely popular follow-on from their Game and Watch machines that children loved in the 1980s. Game Boys included the game Tetris and unleashed the Super Mario Brothers phenomenon, one of the most successful games of all time.

Remember sitting with your finger poised over the 'Record' button of your cassette recorder, waiting for your favourite song to be played on the radio?

Uh, too late ... and you always missed the first few bars!

Or you'd be yelling at everybody to keep quiet when you were recording because you didn't want background noise with the songs.

How easy do kids have it these days? They hear a song they like and it's off to iTunes to download it on to their favourite device and have it, clear and pristine, for instant replay.

Who still has their old cassette recorder because they just couldn't bear to part with it?

A must-have when we were kids

dreamstime

'The Silhouette Man', S. John Ross travelled
Australia cutting out silhouettes

Courtesy of Philip Ross

He was known all around Australia as 'The Silhouette Man'.

His name was S. John Ross and he was a silhouette master with a pair of scissors who started touring the Australian show circuits in about 1948, cutting out silhouettes for the people of Australia.

Over a 60-year period he became a legend at the various shows around Australia and in 2006 he was named an 'Ekka Legend' at the Brisbane Exhibition. S. John Ross became the resident silhouette artist at Sydney's Luna Park in the early 1950s where he worked when not touring. His time at Luna Park came to an end in 1979, following the tragic Ghost Train fire. In more recent years he featured at Sydney's Centrepoint Tower.

S. John Ross died in 2008 at the age of 89.

But his work lives on as thousands of people all around the nation still have their silhouettes, framed and taking pride of place on the mantelpiece.

1967

THE NEWS

Phone 51 0351   Adelaide: Monday, December 18, 1967   5c

No. 13,824—Registered in Australia for transmission by post as a newspaper.

Wher
to loc

Action Line
Crossword, Strip
Finance
Features
Information
Personal
Television

ALL HOPE FOR MR. HOLT GON

Rough sea halt search

MELBOURNE, Today: With a hope of rescue gone, a high organised and concentrated searc resumed at first light this mornin for the body of Australia's Prim Minister, Mr. Harold Holt.

But the search was called off 9.30 a.m. because of heavy rain and rou seas.

About 30 skin divers who were searching the ocean bed were also ordered out of the surf because of treacherous rips and undertows.

One diver was severely gashed when swept on to rocks.

The search will be resumed probably later today when the rough weather is expected to abate.

No administrative action will be taken to appoint a new Prime Minister until either Mr. Holt's body is found or all hope is abandoned.

Already the fear has been expressed by competent opinion that Mr. Holt's body may never be recovered.

Potholes

Beneath the boiling surf are countless deep "potholes" scoured out of the rocky ocean floor.

Sharks, too, are prevalent. A large whaler shark yesterday afternoon took a hooked snapper from a fishing boat line less than a mile from where Mr. Holt vanished without trace.

A nightlong vigil by a Navy search and rescue boat with powerful lights found nothing.

Traffic to the search

THIS picture of Mr. Holt wading from the sea was taken about two months ago at approximately the same place as he disappeared

On the 17 December 1967, as Australians were preparing for early Christmas celebrations, Australia's Prime Minister, Harold Holt, went missing in the surf at Cheviot Beach on Point Napean on the eastern arm of Pt Phillip Bay.

Despite Cheviot Beach being well-known for its strong currents and dangerous rips, Prime Minister Holt decided to take the risk.

Ignoring his friends' pleas not to go swimming, it wasn't long before he disappeared from view. His friends raised the alarm and before long the beach and the water were being searched by a large contingent of police, navy divers, helicopters, Army personnel from nearby Point Nepean, and local volunteers. No trace of Harold Holt could be found and two days later, on 19 December 1967, the Australian Government made an official announcement that Harold Holt was feared drowned and thought to be dead.

It's difficult to imagine, but apparently many people needed a currency converter when Australia swapped to decimal currency in 1966. I don't specifically recall these – apparently many thousands were handed out in an attempt to make sure the currency conversion went smoothly.

Preparations to introduce the new currency had begun in 1963 when the Treasurer at that time, Harold Holt, announced the introduction of legislation to prepare for a changeover to decimal currency. Competitions were held to choose a name for the new currency, with early suggestions including the Royal (suggested by Prime Minister Sir Robert Menzies), the boomer, the roo, the merino, the Eureka and the Anzac.

Decimal currency was finally introduced on 14 February 1966, when dollars and cents replaced the pounds, shillings and pence.

A pocket 1966 decimal currency converter

Courtesy of Jolliday

The News front page from 1967 with the shocking news of the Prime Minister Holt's drowning

Photo by News Ltd/Newspix

Bill was a TV character introduced by the Australian Government in 1966 to teach us all about the new dollars and cents currency that was introduced on 14 February that year.

The TV commercial was made in 1965 for the Decimal Currency Board in preparation for the changeover to decimal currency.

'Dollar Bill and company parade to the repeated strains of the Decimal Currency song, and an exercise in simple addition in pounds, shillings and pence is included to show the virtues of the new system.'

Dollar Bill and company with educational props to explain the currency change over

Photo by News Ltd/Newspix

A pea-green 'shaggin' wagon', with custom paint job on the sides to increase pulling power!

Wikipedia

Who had a 'shaggin' wagon' back in the '70s or '80s?

Shaggin' wagons were basically panel vans, painted in bright colours, fully decked out with a carpeted cargo bay (some had a mattress), a sound system and a built in fridge with murals along the sides, sometimes painted with intricate details.

They had other nicknames too such as 'sin bins', 'mobile virgin conversion units', 'screw canoes', 'Scooby-Doo mobiles', and 'f**k trucks' (you get the drift)! This kind of activity was frequently carried out at the local drive-in. The panel vans would back into the parking bay and everybody knew that 'when the wagons a-rockin' don't come knockin'!

Remember when Mr Whippy first started to sell ice creams in the suburbs and larger towns around Australia? I reckon it would have been mid to late '60s?

During summer school holidays, or on weekends, you'd hear 'Greensleeves' a few streets away and it would get louder as he came closer to your street. Then it was on to try and scrape a few coins together, then a sprint to hopefully catch Mr Whippy before he merrily made his way to the next street.

You could get soft-serve ice creams dipped in chocolate, hundreds and thousands, or topped off with a flake.

By the '90s, many councils began to discourage Mr Whippy in their area because it was felt the vans represented a danger to younger children who, it was feared, would run directly across the road without checking for oncoming traffic.

On a hot summer's night there was no better sound than Greensleeves, alerting you that Mr Whippy was coming with his delicious soft-serve ice creams

Wikipedia, photo David Levinson

Trevor Chappell delivers the infamous underarm
ball to New Zealand's Brian McKechnie

Photo by News Ltd/Newspix

One of the most infamous moments
in modern-day cricket happened on
1 February 1981, when captain of
the Australian Cricket Team, Greg
Chappell, instructed his younger
brother Trevor to bowl an underarm
delivery to New Zealand batsman Brian
McKechnie to prevent him from having
any chance of scoring the six they
needed to tie the match. The action
was legal at the time, but nevertheless
it was seen as being against the spirit of
cricketing fair play and unsportsmanlike.

Australia won the game, but were
booed off the field by spectators. The
New Zealand batsmen walked off in
disgust, McKechnie throwing his bat to
the ground in frustration. McKechnie was
censured for bringing the game of cricket
into disrepute by doing so.

The incident created a feeling of
hostility across the ditch and was roundly
criticised by commentators of the game
all around the world.

A 1950s 'ice chest' used for keeping perishables cold before we all had fridges. In front is a set of ice tongs that the ice man used to carry the big block of ice

Courtesy of the Image Kid (http://imgkid.com)

I vividly recall my parent's first kitchen with lino on the floor, the old kitchen cabinet with the mantel wireless on top and the ice chest in the corner.

I'm trying to recall when we got our first fridge. I believe it would have been in the mid-50s and until then the ice man called every couple of days. He would carry a big block of ice inside with the ice tongs and place it in the top of the ice chest.

The other thing I remember is that the dish that lived under the ice chest had to be emptied regularly as it caught all the water as the ice slowly melted. I recall it was a job that, as one of the older members of the family, and being the boy and supposedly stronger than my sisters – fell to me! Good training too because if I ever forgot, then I'd have to clean up the mess.

#37
FACT

Aerobics exploded in Australia in the 1980s. Remember the Jane Fonda Workout video? Lycra, leg warmers and 'Let's Get Physical' made aerobics one of the top three sports in Australia by the end of the decade and helped create today's gym culture. But you don't see many fluoro pink sweatbands anymore.

Hard at work in the milk bar, 1946

Photo by News Ltd/Newspix

When you were growing up where was your favourite milk bar?

Those were the times when you could get a milkshake and a sandwich at your local milk bar or deli, which was more like a café than the convenience stores of today.

They were generally family run businesses that also sold homemade hamburgers, sandwiches, pies and pasties, sweets, smallgoods, bread and general food items.

Once upon a time, the local milk bar/deli was the place to gather after school, or after work, or a meeting place on a Saturday night.

I doubt that teenagers today would gather at a milk bar, most these days would rather go to the pub, not that we didn't frequent pubs as well, although I think that you had to be 21 before you could legally drink back then (I'm talking '50s and '60s).

A NewSouth book

Published by
NewSouth Publishing
University of New South Wales Press Ltd
University of New South Wales
Sydney NSW 2052
AUSTRALIA
newsouthpublishing.com

© Bob Byrne 2015
First published 2015

10 9 8 7 6 5 4 3 2 1

National Library of Australia
Cataloguing-in-Publication entry
Creator: Byrne, Bob, author.
Title: Australia remember when / Bob Byrne.
ISBN: 9781742234564 (paperback)
Subjects: Australia–History.
           Australia–Social life and customs.
Dewey Number: 994

DESIGN Di Quick
COVER DESIGN Katy Wall

FRONT COVER Attendants 'servicing' an EH Holden motor
car at a service station in Bulleen. Museum Victoria. Reg.
No: MM 55244; It wasn't a Saturday night if you missed
'Hey Hey It's Saturday' with Daryl, Ossie and the gang.
Courtesy of Channel Nine; Chocolate Crackles. Courtesy
of Copha, a registered trademark of Peerless Foods Pty
Ltd; Children playing in the school playground in 1954–55.
Museum Victoria. Reg. No: MM 104103
BACK COVER Beach inspector Aub Laidlaw inspects a
bikini to make sure it meets 'public decency' standards at
Bondi, 16 November 1958. Photo by News Ltd/Newspix;
Before suburban swimming pools, kids used to keep cool
in one of these. Museum Victoria. Reg. No: MM 110513;
'Dame Edna Everage', Sydney, 1983. Photo by News Ltd/
Newspix; Michael and Linday Chamberlain talking to the
media in 1980 soon after a dingo had taken their baby
Azaria. Photo by News Ltd/Newspix; A pea-green shaggin'
wagon with a custom paint job on the sides to increase
pulling power! Wikipedia

PRINTER Everbest, China

This book is printed on paper using fibre supplied from
plantation or sustainably managed forests.